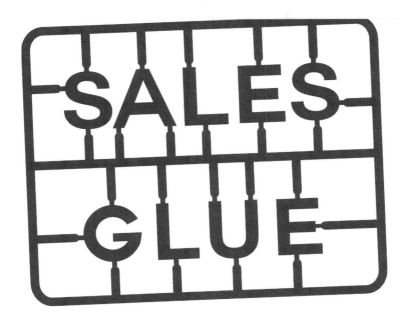

THE VITAL INGREDIENT THAT
MAKES SALES SUCCESS STICK

MATT SYKES

R∃THINK PRESS

First published in Great Britain 2017
by Rethink Press (www.rethinkpress.com)
© Copyright Matt Sykes

Dedicated to Sue and Ollie whose blind faith in my journey allowed these words to be written.

Contents

Preface

We all know lots of helpful things that we don't always do anything with.

Sales Glue was written to help sales professionals tap into that perfectly normal phenomenon. It is the culmination of over twenty years of real-life sales experience and brings together what I believe to be some incredibly helpful and practical sales advice but more importantly, it will show ways in which you can take what you know and create helpful and consistent action.

Within the chapters are strategies designed to show you how to take the sales skills you already have and those you may learn from the book to create sales habits by linking them to the way we think. We've got a great piece of kit in our heads and understanding more about how the brain functions, both how it can help us perform and at times hindering us, will allow you to get even more consistency from your sales activities.

I've kept this book as concise as possible as I want you to take on the advice and put it into practice straight away. At the end of each chapter you will find tips called 'sticking points. You'll also find quotes from some of the 'greats' from the world of Sales and Personal Development and the occasional cartoon. These aren't space-fillers, they are learning tools designed to help you process the information. Our brain can often struggle with new information because it is trying so hard to understand the concepts on offer in the pages and at the same time put the advice into practical application. The chapter summary points, inspirational quotes and cartoons are all additional tools to reinforce the learning and help you make your selling skills stick.

By design, *Sales Glue* is not a long read. I listen to a lot of podcasts which specialise in Sales and Marketing and one recently suggested that as many as 85% of all self-help books have never been completed cover to cover. Partly for that reason and because I appreciate that you may have a huge array of things challenging you for your time and attention, the chapters are direct and to the point – I want you to finish my book.

Sales Glue is dedicated to all sales professionals out there today engaged in life's daily grind and hustle. It's a profession that is often misunderstood and sometimes taken for granted. Without sales people, the ability to transfer goods and services from one person to another would be significantly challenged. As twenty-year plus sales professional and an active member of the profession of selling today, I want you to be confident that the things I share in this book are all being used to help me on a daily basis in both my professional and personal life.

This book is ultimately a self-help guide that is designed to not only help you find ways to sell more to more people more often, but can be used to create emotional resilience and inspire you to become even more fulfilled when the working day comes to a close and your 'you' time begins.

I hope you enjoy it.

Introduction

Let's start with a question; I believe it's a big one.

What has prompted you to read these words?

There could be a variety of different answers of course, but taking the time to reflect and think about it allows you the opportunity to uncover the reasons why you are. Questions are the life-blood of sales. They create a platform for discussion that when done well, can ultimately lead to a solution. Good and relevant questions help establish a need or identify a problem or pain that someone would like to solve. When we solve the problem, we make the sale. Put simply, questions are the answer.

So why are you reading *Sales Glue*?

One thing's likely: you recognise the difference between being responsible and taking responsibility. You're taking accountability for how your future turns out by investing in yourself to learn new skills. You could feel you have more potential to give, and right at this moment in your career, you may be struggling to see how you can develop it. You're possibly curious to know what you can do with it, and where it could take you.

If you're anything like me, you'll believe passionately that being independently minded is good. It is the edge you have. It's the starting point for creating and building an advantage in your sales role. *Sales Glue* has been written for people like you.

Maybe you've just completed your first ten thousand hours and you're ready to make your next career move. Possibly you're an established Sales Manager with your own team who you want to support and mentor to higher levels of performance and achievement. You could be a Sales Director looking for inspiration and advice to take the leap, go out alone and create your own business.

Either way, you will almost certainly benefit from your investment in time to read this book because it has been written by someone who has been in each of those roles. Like you, I have experienced the challenges and opportunities that make up the most important profession there is – the profession of selling, and I continue to do so. Take on the many ideas and strategies in *Sales Glue* and you could shift from where you are right now - to being a consistent, high achieving sales expert, enjoying the benefits that come with sales success.

Now I accept that there are plenty of books out there promising to teach you how to get more customers and grow your business, each with their own unique take on the noble art of selling. I own many of these books, and while they all offer ways in which to achieve sales success and are worthy of a place on my bookshelf, the reality is that achieving sales success, although simple, simply isn't easy. In fact, it's hard as hell.

> ### *The harder you work, the luckier you get.*
>
> **Gary Player**

What's interesting is most people know that all the help they'll ever need to be successful at selling is waiting for them in today's 24/7 online world of YouTube, but some have yet to tap into it fully. Jim Rohn once said 'Everything you need for your better future and success has already been written. And guess what? It's all available.' It's a bitter sweet reminder that sometimes all they need to do to become a student of sales and perpetually improve is be more exposed to what's available more often. Perhaps they have been reading, watching and listening to the online sales university, but are not putting it into practice each day. This book could well point them to the missing ingredient they've been lacking.

In my experience, most people in life have latent potential, but few make a conscious decision to release it. You could be one of the few who do. You had a choice and you chose to read *Sales Glue*, in which you will find over thirty sales tips that you can put to work today. I genuinely want you to reach your true sales potential and I hope that the following pages will help take you on a journey towards that.

My secret to sales success lies in taking the advice in the pages that follow and applying it consistently until it becomes a habit. As Jeffrey Gitomer, author of *Little Red Book of Selling* (over 4million copies sold at time of writing) reminds us:

> ### *If you are willing to work hard for 20 years, you can become an instant overnight sales success!*
>
> **Jeffrey Gitomer**

Success comes only after you've built a reputation, gained credibility, built trusted relationships, experienced the don'ts, mastered the dos and put in the hours. If you're willing to do the hard work, then sales is easy, but there's no short cut and, dare I say it, very little new in the world of sales training. However, I can reassure you that every sales book I've ever read has contained at least one piece of information that I was seriously able to consider and, in most cases, translate into my daily sales behaviour, which significantly justified the return on the cover price.

This book provides one consistent piece of additional learning: the ability to help you take what you read, apply it and make it stick. Sales professionals already know how to sell. They just may not know how to do it regularly, and there's a big difference between knowing and doing. Right now, there's something stopping them from taking what they already know and making it a habit.

Sales Glue is going to show you exactly how to do this.

The very first sale a sales person has to make is to sell themselves. If the customer doesn't buy them, they won't buy their product, and if the sales person doesn't buy themselves, they won't put themselves into opportunities and situations that will bring them sales success. They need to take responsibility for their own sales education and master possibly the most under-valued and over-estimated skill on the planet – helping people decide to buy what they have.

If you are reading this book while in a sales role through choice with an expectation to improve your skills and a burning desire to create habits that will achieve sales success, then it can help you get there. I have shared my experience from over twenty years in the sales industry and linked it to advice from some of the best sales advocates in the world. I've studied many of them and see it as my obligation to share with you anything and everything I can to help you succeed, irrespective of whether the advice comes from me or from other people. Within the pages that follow are words of wisdom, sales strategies and tips that work.

A word of caution: the process of earning sales success is challenging, occasionally frustrating and not for under-achievers. Some give up before achieving their goal because the challenge is too great, or the rewards do not come quickly or consistently enough. You probably already have many of the tools you need to succeed; you may simply need to learn how to use them more effectively. This book will help you to do that.

The world of selling is changing beyond all recognition. The dominance of social media is a temptation to every sales professional who finds it hard to grow interdependent face-to-face relationships. We are closer than ever to a sales person being replaced by a Buy Now button on a website. Look at what Tesla Motors is doing: there's no negotiation on price, all that takes place on-line. Instead the Tesla sales rep devotes the customer interaction experience to instructing the buyer on where they can charge Tesla cars, the size of government electric car incentives, and how much they can expect to pay in electricity versus gas. If this is the future of how we buy cars, maybe the on-line shopping experience is a clear and present danger to those who choose selling as a career. So, what can we do to mitigate that threat? How can we become so irreplaceable that we, the sales professionals, cannot be replaced?

Some of what you read in the pages that follow may well be known to you. Why wouldn't it be? The best sales training has succeeded in the past, so why change a winning formula? This book, however, could be your moment to decide to make a change in how you use that knowledge, to master your existing sales skills and create a new way of working that will raise your sales success to new heights, distancing you from your competition and bringing real value to your customer.

Ready to go there?

Chapter One

If You're Anything Like Me

If there's one conclusion I've come to in the last twenty years of working in the sales industry, it's that most sales professionals are capable of achieving more than they do. With the right education and regular application of the things they've learnt, they have the ability to over-achieve in sales, bring a greater return on their employer's investment and reach their true potential. I talk from experience: I spent eighteen years working in a corporate sales environment, doing a good job, hitting targets, winning new business, keeping clients happy and pacifying them when things didn't go well. I was well-paid by my employer, but, if I'm honest, I was doing just enough to keep ahead of the average achievers in the sales team, making sure that the pay cheque arrived every month. I'd fallen victim to the thing which motivates most people at some point in their working lives – comfort.

While I genuinely believe that most sales professionals are missing out on the chance to improve their skills and subsequently their success, I am no longer in that category. In deciding to read this book, in all likelihood, neither are you.

Brian Tracy, the American sales expert and motivational speaker, said, 'You don't pick a career in sales, you fall backwards into it.' Maybe that's true for most, but after leaving school aged sixteen, I chose, much to my parent's frustration, a job selling shoes in a high street store ahead of an apprenticeship in printing.

On my first day, the store manager explained to me, 'Our job is not to sell shoes, our job is to sell shoe trees.' I remember thinking at the time that he was nuts. Why wouldn't we sell shoes? It was, after all, a shoe shop. However, as I watched him throughout my first day, I quickly became transfixed by his ability to engage with people who came into the store. He would strike up a conversation with customers with a confidence and sincerity which put them at ease and helped them trust him. With a few well-chosen phrases like: 'How long did your last pair of shoes last?' or 'If you wear shoes in the wet, stopping the leather from cracking as it dries will extend their life', he helped those customers to make a decision that was good for them. I was amazed – the shoe trees were literally walking out of the store! It was my first experience of real selling.

While I failed miserably at selling shoe trees in the early weeks of my career, I became fascinated by the art of selling – or, as we now regard it, helping people to buy. I realised there was a right way and a wrong to sell, and most of it hinged on engaging with people in such a way that I could find out what they wanted, hoping that what they wanted was what I had. Watching my store manager sell countless shoe trees, which in some cases were as expensive as the shoes themselves, I felt a fire to succeed ignite within me.

My journey into the 'people business' stalled when I swapped polish for printing ink and succumbed to the printing apprenticeship. However, my addiction to engaging with people and learning how to build rapport never went away, and over the next fifteen years I found myself flirting with the art once again, selling gym memberships, de-humidifiers, protein supplements and even advertising space before finally settling on an eighteen-year career selling packaging to clients all over Europe. In my final year in corporate employment, I was European Sales Director, responsible for a €70million sales revenue portfolio, in charge of a sales team operating across the UK and Benelux.

While I thoroughly enjoyed every day of my employment, working with great colleagues and customers, I always felt I was capable of achieving more. Maybe you are feeling a bit like I did then. I was keen to learn, but while every other department was being trained to within an inch of its life, the sales team's skillset always seemed to get neglected. I recall attending a two day 'Introduction to Selling' course in my first year, but beyond a number of negotiation training days, nothing more was provided to help me improve my sales skills.

What I find fascinating as I talk to sales professionals all over the UK and Europe is that many organisations adopt the same approach. For some, it's far more important to train someone in the art of negotiation on the basis that *'we'll no doubt be hammered down on price again this year and we'd better be ready for it'* rather than training sales skills which position value as the buying driver, thus usually avoiding a discussion on price at all. Net result – no negotiation.

I now run my own training company specialising in performance improvement. On my very first day in self-employment, despite having spent the previous eighteen years as a sales professional, I quickly came to the conclusion that I'd forgotten how to sell. I had a great product, an office, a phone and email, but no customers. I had to find a way of helping new clients to realise that they needed what I had to offer.

The big problem I had was that despite successfully managing a team of European sales people and negotiating multi-million pound contracts, through lack of practice, I'd lost some of the core basic skills of selling – I'd forgotten how to sell shoe trees! If I was to make my new business successful, I needed to rediscover those skills, and quickly.

Fast-forward to today and the art of selling is no longer a mystery to me. It is after all a relatively simple process when followed meticulously. By 'meticulously', I mean every time I enter into the sale process, it leads to a decision and most of the time a sale. The following pages reveal that process and give you tips from my mentors from the world of sales excellence.

Some trainers say that you have to have done the 'hard yards' and 'got the battle scars' to be able to teach people how to sell, and I agree with them about the hard yards. Provided you've spent at least five years in the sales industry, you have more than enough experience to apply what I will share with you and shift your sales performance to the next level without getting scarred at all.

At this point, I must give you a word of warning. The reason why most sales people are failing to reach their true potential relates to one fundamental skill that I've learnt – there's a direct link between how they think and how their sales success plays out. In short, they can have the best sales skills and behaviour out there, but if they fail to have a mindset which allows them to exploit those skills, they'll always fall short.

> ### *Attitude not aptitude determines altitude.*
> **Zig Ziglar**

I cannot emphasise enough how important your personal psychology is. To be able to motivate yourself when things are going well is easy, but what will separate you from the rest is how you maintain motivation when times are tough.

Without people selling the products and services of companies, there would be no companies, simple as that. While we may not always like to face the music when our product or service fails, we empathise with the customer, accept and apologise, and then re-build the relationship so that trust allows new sales to flow.

Given the political and economic landscape in the world, things could well become a whole lot tougher in future for those whose job it is to generate new business. When you learn how to create laser-like focus, discover a self-belief and confidence which protects and elevates you, are clear on your outcomes and have a framework and daily discipline to achieve them, then you distance yourself from the rest. That is where this book will take you.

The following chapters will give you help, advice and exercises designed to develop your sales behaviour and mindset to allow you to reach your full sales potential. If you want more new customers, and more sales from the customers you already have, please read on. I want to help you find the sort of success and opportunity that is out there, just waiting for you to take it. We live in truly remarkable times – never in our history has it been so easy to excel at the profession of sales. With market uncertainty comes fear and paralysis, and this is your opportunity to expand into the spaces inevitably left vacant. The internet and social media especially platforms like LinkedIn allow you a global stage to perform on if you're the sort of person who wants to enjoy a career and life full of achievement which matches your true potential.

STICKING POINTS

■ **Approach the following chapters with an open mind.** Take the time to consider the key principles and methodologies presented to you. Even if some seem strange at first, I promise that each one has been proven.

■ **Invest in a journal and take lots of notes.** The more you write, the more the learning will stick. The ideas in this book may prompt you to think of other specific opportunities and applications for your sales role, so write them down too. They're gold.

■ **Put into practice what you read and commit to creating a culture of repetition.** It takes less than sixty days to make a habit and just like training any muscle, you need to work at it, consistently.

Chapter Two

Follow the Leader

Many people believe that the greatest ever sales book is *Think and Grow Rich* by Napoleon Hill. Written in 1937 following a directive from business magnate and philanthropist Andrew Carnegie to seek out the success tips of the good and the great at that time, the book has sold over 70million copies, and the advice it offers is so successful it is often still recited by speakers at conferences and events today.

If you want to get really successful in a certain field, find someone who's achieved success and follow what they did. This is after all what all the sales greats did themselves – they followed, worked with or were guided by a coach or mentor: someone with the experience and ability to nurture and guide them along a path towards improvement.

I have a professional mentor whom I meet with regularly, and aside from the advice, experience and opportunities that relationship has provided, it is so beneficial to get someone else's opinion on matters that affect my personal performance. This book would probably not have been written if I hadn't met my first mentor, Gavin Drake, a psychological performance specialist, in 2008. He instilled a belief within me that anything is possible if you set your mind to it, and no doubt he had his own mentor giving him that same advice some years before we met.

I believe that while a good teacher can help you achieve success through sharing knowledge and wisdom with you, a good mentor can increase it by ensuring that knowledge is turned into habitual action through regular exposure to accountability and motivation. If it's important and contributes to your success, a mentor will keep you on task.

However, having a mentor doesn't always mean physically finding someone to guide you (although I recommend doing so if possible), especially if you're unsure about the correct qualities required to meet your needs right now. To start with, if there's an area of your sales acumen you feel could benefit from improving, type a key word – let's say 'motivation' – into YouTube. Within seconds, you'll have an army of virtual coaches and mentors ready to advise you, and you'll normally find that the ones with the highest 'view count' are offering the best advice.

My first 'virtual' sales coach was Tom Hopkins, the American real-estate salesman turned multi-millionaire sales trainer, and the knowledge I extracted from his books, videos and audios has been invaluable on my journey of mastering the art of selling. There are many words of wisdom I could share with you in this book, but I'll start with Tom's approach to the 'Three must haves to be great in sales':

1. You have to believe totally in your product – would you buy what you sell?

Take some time to reflect on what your product does and how it helps people and make a list of the benefits they get from owning it. If you are not totally committed to your product or service, there's a real danger your lack of confidence will show in your communication with your customers, and that will significantly hinder your ability to help people decide to buy what you have. If you're not convinced, you cannot convince.

2. Find qualified people who want to buy what you have and professionally help them towards saying 'Yes'

The need to have an effective lead generation system and a full pipeline is fundamental to your success. Do you already have a structured process in place that will drive prospects to you? Are you clear which prospects are right for you? Are you adding new prospects to your sales funnel all the time or only when you run low? Think about how you feel when sales are slow and, conversely, what life's like when you have so much potential business you are struggling to see everyone who wants to buy from you.

3. Help people make decisions that are good for them

Tom's mantra is always to make it about the other person. Let them see and feel that you have their best interests at heart. When buyers clearly see your conviction in your product and the benefits that it will bring in making their lives easier, then they are better placed to decide to buy what you have on offer.

The combination of these three qualities helps you towards the title of 'expert', and that is a quality you need if people are going to buy from you. The phrase 'expert advisor' has been used in the field of sales training for years for obvious reasons – no one wants to buy from someone who isn't an expert in what they are offering. However, I've bought from 'experts' in the past who have ultimately given me the wrong advice. I take part of the blame for that, but the bottom-line is I no longer trust them and won't be buying from them again. Neither will I refer them to other people, so they ultimately lose.

Here's a key point: rather than being an 'expert advisor' who may only get one sale, strive to become a 'trusted advisor' who builds a relationship geared towards a lifetime of sales.

People will be more inclined to take advice from people they trust, and provided your advice is authentic, including enough facts, substance and information to help your prospect make the right decision, then everyone wins. Even if your advice ultimately results in the prospect not buying from you this time, you still win.

Some sales people will struggle with this last point because the buyer closes on a no, but they are failing to see the bigger picture of lifetime value – repeat business that can potentially be generated over the lifetime of the relationship. Not only that, I will always refer trusted advisors who have helped me to people who put their trust in me. Trust between buyer and seller means sales can always happen – without trust, it's over. There is one further progression we can make which can move us beyond the position of trusted advisor and closer to our destination of sales success – the ability to be liked. Being liked by your prospect eclipses even trust in my opinion. Trust can't be created if the person you're in front of doesn't like you.

The final piece of Tom Hopkins' advice I want share with you is one of the most important things I've learnt in the context of selling:

> *People only ever buy two things: a solution to a problem or an improvement to what they've already got.*

This message is so powerful yet so often missed by sales people. I think back to my earlier years of selling packaging and wince at my naivety – the number of times I tried (and failed) to sell products that didn't tick either of these two boxes. I used to think that my product was the 'main event', the reason why the other person wanted to buy – trust me, it was not. People don't care what you have to sell; they just want what's in it for them, and what's usually in it for them is a solution to a problem. Run a check on your product right now: does it solve your customer's problem or is it an improvement on what they currently have?

Harvard Business School Professor Theodore Levitt supports this when he says:

> ***People don't want to buy a quarter-inch drill; they want to buy a quarter-inch hole.***

Most people in sales have heard this quote. It sums up the difference between features and benefits and the need to identify somebody's problem.

Think about your own situation right now. Let's assume that your need is to expand your sales skills knowledge. It just so happens that reading a sales book is an easy and affordable way to provide the solution, hence you buy a book. It is the right fit for your need.

We'll cover more on this later in the book as it is the key to being a master at selling and understanding the importance of psychology and emotion in sales.

As the famous Jeffrey Gitomer quote says:

> ### *People don't like to be sold – but they love to buy.*

Apart from those of us in the sales profession who actually enjoy being sold to – let's be honest, we have such an affinity with other sales people that we are an easy close, most people run for the hills at the sight of a sales person. They feel they are about to be tricked or conned out of their hard-earned cash by the fast-talking, sharp-suited sleaze-ball. Emotion plays such a big part in our purchasing experience that if we feel we are being rushed or pushed into buying something, we subconsciously act to defend ourselves – in other words, we find a way to stop the process and head for the exit. It's human nature, and the sooner we as sales people recognise this, the easier it becomes to sell something.

When people object to whatever it is that they are being sold, it is a clear signal that they don't see enough value in the deal on offer – too much drill and not enough hole. Either the sales person hasn't provided enough of the right information to help them see the benefit or the sequence used to engage with the prospect was in the wrong order or lacked something. Quite often it's the words a sales person uses that bring the emotion of fear into the minds of the buyers and can derail the sale.

I'm always fascinated by shop assistants who come up to me, invade my space and say, 'Are you OK there? Do you need some help?'

While maybe I should be grateful that they've shown an interest in me in the first place, I can't help thinking how much better the feeling would be for a shopper, and therefore how much better their response would be, if the shop assistant said, 'That's a nice shirt you're looking at. What sort of occasion would you wear that for?'

STICKING POINTS

- **Most sales skills training can be found on the internet.** Pick an area of sales improvement you are looking for and type it into YouTube. You'll find plenty of good advice on how to improve your sales skills, and a few examples of how not to do it.

- **Strive to become a trusted advisor.** What five skills could you improve to help you achieve this status?

- **Talk only about the features of your product which are important to your customers, the benefits.** Write down three features and list the three benefits that these features create, then you can incorporate these benefits into your sales discussions with buyers.

Chapter Three

Fall in Love With the Process

There's a quote that I reflect on daily. It acts as a compass for my day to day activity in both my business and personal life, and it comes from *The 7 Habits of Highly Effective People*, the international best-seller by Steven Covey;

> ### *Begin with the end in mind.*
> **Steven Covey**

While the book itself is essentially a guide to productive and constructive self-leadership, this quote sums up exactly what is needed if you are to succeed and reach your true potential in life. When you consider your destination and then 'reverse engineer' all of the activity required to get there, you create a map – a psychological framework that identifies the sequence of the steps you need to travel along.

I place huge importance on having a constructive psychology to drive my sales activity, and I will show you the process and sequence I go through not only to develop great sales behaviour but to drive that behaviour every day. As I mentioned in the last chapter, I met my first mentor Gavin Drake in 2008. At the time, he was already a successful Performance Improvement Specialist working with businesses and sports professionals across the UK and Europe. I attended his Mindspan training programme, and what I'm about to share with you from that programme literally transformed my life. It is the single most important thing I've ever learnt and has become the process I use every day of my life.

It's called the Thinking Cycle.

Thoughts. Psychology tells us that every day, all day, we are engaged in thoughts. Most of these thoughts happen automatically, driven by the subconscious part of our mind.

As you read these words, however, it's the conscious part of your brain, that is being used to think about their meaning and decide whether it has value for you.

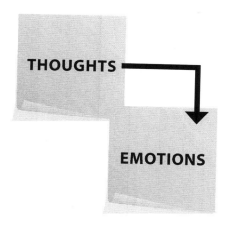

Emotions. The way we think about a specific thing, person or situation will have a significant impact on how we feel about those things – our emotions. If someone reading this book is saying to themselves, 'What is the point of this stuff? Why did I bother to pick up this book?' the emotions they are probably experiencing are frustration, boredom, even anger.

In contrast, the person who's saying to themselves, 'This is a good read, it looks like there's real value in this for me' will probably be feeling an opposite set of emotions – interest, curiosity and engagement. This is hugely significant for step number three.

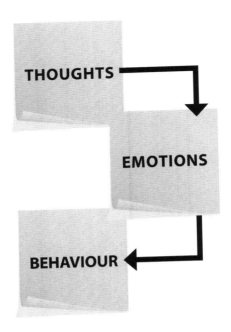

Behaviour. The way that we feel and the emotions that we experience are significant drivers of how we act – our behaviour. Because our actions and behaviours are driven by how we feel, the reader who feels negatively about the book may decide to stop reading, put the book down and possibly spend the next hour feeling annoyed with themselves for wasting their time and money. But the person who is thinking and feeling positively will be far more likely to continue to read, possibly making notes or highlighting the text for future reference.

Now the Thinking Cycle comes to life. At this point, though, before I complete it with the fourth and final element, I'd like you to consider this: I believe that in addition to our interior world – the place from which we go about our day-to-day lives

– there is the outside world. We also participate in the outside world, but it's a place over which we have little or no control.

For example, we can't control the weather. We can't control our customers either. How about our boss, or the $/£ exchange rate? I accept that we can have a level of influence over these things, but we can't fully control them. Yet while we can't control our external environment, and by this I mean what goes on around us in the world, we now know (because psychology tells us) that we have more control than we realise over our internal lives. How we think is driving how we feel. It's those feelings which are impacting how we behave, react and respond, and all of that has a massive influence over point number four of the Thinking Cycle: our outcomes.

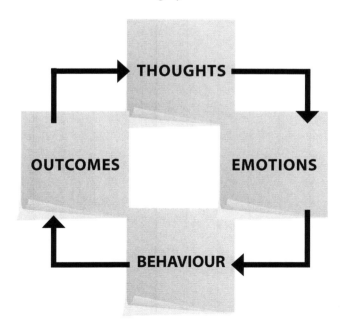

Outcomes. If we are looking to experience more positive outcomes in the world of sales, such as more qualified prospects, more sales from existing customers and more new customer sales, we need to make sure we have an attitude, mindset or personal psychology which drives the emotions and behaviours required to create them. Thinking in a less than constructive way is likely to produce the opposite outcome.

In our day-to-day sales life, we are always engaged in a thinking cycle – we were yesterday, we are right now, we will be tomorrow. We are constantly thinking, feeling, behaving and creating, and then thinking about each outcome, and around we go again. We now know that there is a direct link between what we habitually do mentally and how our sales performances turn out.

So if you want more successful sales outcomes, it's about ensuring you adopt a constructive and positive sales psychology every day. The positive feelings that arise when we think about sales success will drive us to take more productive action towards it.

> ### It's not what you think about that's crucial, it's the way that you think about what you think about that's crucial.
>
> **Mindspan**

Just like a helpful mental process, selling has a sequence which needs to be followed if a successful outcome for both buyer and seller is to take place. It's a little bit like marriage – we meet someone, and while there has been the odd case in Vegas where a wedding followed two hours and a bottle of tequila later, the norm is that we go through a number of steps before we book the church and ask Auntie Ethel to buy a hat. We spend quality time in the other person's company, finding out all about them – their interests, hobbies, likes and dislikes. We meet them for dinner and later, if it still feels right, we move in together, propose marriage, and bingo!

Sales is exactly the same. The Sales Sequence is widely known but rarely used with discipline, and as a result, I'm afraid, most sales professionals are simply winging it. Sure, they might achieve one sale without it, but their chances of selling more are reduced if they don't adopt a sales sequence all of the time. Which area of their delivery will they measure and correct if they don't know which part of the sequence let them down?

This simple diagram explains the Sales Sequence for you:

Following the sequence through each step, you will gain the confidence to know that the further you get along the process, the more likely you are to get a decision that is good for you and equally good for the buyer. The danger of not following the sequence is obvious. If you jump from qualifying your prospect to providing your solution, don't be surprised if they object because you haven't even discovered their problem yet. Treating each step as not just mandatory, but also enjoyable, you will understand your buyer, ensuring your product or service solves their needs. This will limit the number of objections you get and pretty much guarantees the prospect will buy.

I've seen and read about many different versions and interpretations of the Sales Sequence, and I'd like to share an excellent version from Ben Chaib of Sell and Succeed, who has a great sequence called the S8 Formula. This is not only easy to commit to memory, but will also bring an extra dimension to your sales skills.

Let's take a look at it:

1. Share. Build trust, show an interest and create common ground so your prospect feels comfortable. Rapport allows you to ask great questions so they share information with you.

2. Suitability. Once you've gone through Share and understand their needs, you will be able to decide whether they are suitable and qualified to receive a proposal. Ask more questions about their specific need and detail how your product can bring value to them. The more they share about their problem, the more they are confirming to themselves that they need a solution.

3. Significance. Uncover their problem and understand what it's costing them. Find out what the pain of doing nothing would be and identify what benefits would be available to them if a solution could be found. If you introduce monetary value at this point it will help in the next steps of the sequence. What is the cost of this problem to them or their business?

4. Stretch. Help the buyer imagine what the future will look like and the value making a change will bring to them. Again, it's important to pinpoint a monetary value and get them to verbalise what they would do with that cash. Ask them how they would feel and how their business would improve as a result.

5. Select. Here is your opportunity to get the prospect to decide that they want you to help them. If you ask how others have (or haven't) found a solution for them, the prospect will explain for themselves why others haven't done what you have done, or could do.

6. Spend. Identify the prospect's willingness to invest. Literally ask the prospect to calculate the total saving that the solution you've jointly found will provide over the next ten years, which puts a realistic value on what you have. If they are willing to invest to return that saving, the prospect will accept and pay for your solution.

7. Start. Here you confirm when the client wants to realise the outcome then simply reverse engineer the process to the start date. This gives the project a sense of urgency, given that every month they delay costs them money.

8. Solution. This is where you take all the information from the previous seven steps to get the prospect to confirm what the problem is and what the solution is. Then you explain how your product meets all their needs and you gain their commitment.

I love this sequence because it places a monetary saving into the discussion, which creates real focus and makes the need for a decision that much greater. As sales professionals, our job is ultimately to get people to make a decision that's right for both them and us, and avoiding losing money is a good problem for a prospect to solve.

There's plenty of evidence to suggest that the brain reacts more strongly towards things it deems to be problematic – it goes right back to prehistoric times when we needed to be aware of pending attacks from predators. So whilst I hope none of your prospects feels they are under attack in your presence, allowing them to focus more on the problem than the solution is tapping into the way the brain naturally functions.

Traditional sales behaviour focuses on presenting the solution, but maybe we can improve our results by spending more time helping prospects see the problem that's in front of them. It exists, we aren't being negative or trying to scare them – we simply want them to see it clearly so they can find a way, with our help, to solve it.

Every sales professional and manager of a sales team needs to know at any one time where their top prospects are in the sales cycle. I strongly encourage you to adopt this approach today as it will bring real benefit in terms of clarity and productivity, and ultimately deliver a higher conversion rate. Whether its via your CRM, a spreadsheet on your laptop or tablet, or a wipe board in your office, make it visible and make yourself accountable.

STICKING POINTS

■ **Take a photo or make a copy of the Thinking Cycle and look at it daily.** It will help you adopt a productive thought process for the day ahead and remind you how much control you have over your results.

■ **Create the Sales Sequence on a spreadsheet and plot where each of your top fifteen prospects are within it.** Decide what you need to do to pass them through to the referrals stage successfully. Measure your success rate and identify at which part of the sequence you encountered issues, then learn from them.

■ **Reflect on the S8 Formula and seek to build stretch and monetary value into your discussions with your prospects.** Help them see the financial consequences of not taking action with you so they make a decision that's right for them. Focus more on the problem rather than the solution and you'll help them more.

Chapter Four

Build It, but They Won't Come

We talked in Chapter Two about mentors and how they can help you bring transformational change in your results, like becoming more creative with your selling style and keeping motivated to stay on task even when times are tough. One such mentor is Peter Thompson. He is, without doubt, a brilliant salesman. It's important to point out that Peter doesn't actually know me; I came across him when researching a solution for a sales question that I had.

Each week, Peter sends me an email containing words of advice, and every now and then, he'll send one with a call to action to buy something from him. I'm just one of thousands on his email database list, but Peter has earned the right to keep me on his list by the way he engages with me. We can learn so much from his approach – let me share a few tips in this chapter.

On my very first day of self-employment, I started to value the importance of having a lead generation system as I simply didn't have one. Thinking back to my career selling packaging, when sales kept coming from some magical place called 'repeat order kingdom', I never placed enough value on what has to happen to generate a lead and how that lead subsequently becomes an order.

A business needs to position lead generation very much front and centre within its list of priorities. Even if the task is held elsewhere within the company you work for, I recommend you make it your mission to understand who is doing it and how they are doing it, because the day you take your eye off it is the day you sign your professional death warrant.

"Esther...have Sales do that thing where customers place orders would you?"

If you work for yourself, you will understand that last point. Too many companies put on the lights in the morning, open the door and wait for the customers to walk in – 'build it and they will come' is as dangerous a mission statement in sales as offering discounts to 'brand new customers only'. Build it, yes, but then go out and take massive amounts of action to help people see the value in what you have for them. Help them get involved somehow.

This is essentially what Peter is doing each week with his emails, and the many other techniques he uses in his lead generation system. This book is exactly that – its intention is to help you improve as a sales person, and in return, I hope trust and credibility will build between us. You may then decide to tell others about this book and possibly invest in some future sales training with my company.

Whether it's friends and family, LinkedIn contacts, email marketing, a social media campaign, referrals, posts and blogs, networking or, dare I say, picking up the phone and talking to people, the key message here is to take action to solve the biggest sales killer of them all: obscurity. If people don't know you, they can't grow you. If you haven't got a process in place to fill your pipeline in a long-term, systematic way, you are operating in the world of luck, and true sales professionals prefer to plan ahead.

> ### *Prospecting... find the man with the problem.*
> **Benjamin Friedman**

As discussed in the Sales Sequence, lead generation results in qualified prospects who are the lifeblood of our business. How many qualified prospects we need and how much prospecting to do is governed by our sales pipeline. This is another fundamental process which all highly successful sales professionals use.

A brilliant example of how to start with the end in mind is to commit to building our sales pipeline and filling it every day. We begin with our annual sales revenue target – the value which we have committed to delivering to our organisation each year. Let's use a hypothetical example of £150,000.

Next we need to calculate what the average order value is for the products and services we sell. Let's go with £3,000.

We then want to understand what our conversion rate is based on how many qualified prospects end up buying our products and services. Let's say we convert one customer from every three prospects.

Finally, we calculate the number of pre-qualified people, sometimes referred to as 'suspects', we need to talk to before we confirm that they qualify for what we have to offer and become prospects. We'll go with two suspects translating into one qualified prospect.

Armed with this information, we can calculate that we need to speak with six suspects each week if we are to achieve our annual sales revenue target. The following breakdown explains it:

Sales revenue target (A) = £150,000

Average order value (B) = £3,000

Number of individual sales (C) = £150,000 (A)/£3,000 (B) = 50

Qualified prospects needed for each order (D) = 3

Total number of qualified prospects for target (E) = 50 (C) x 3 (D) = 150

Number of suspects to get one qualified prospect (F) = 2

Total number of suspects needed to contact (G) = 150 (E) x 2 (F) = 300

How many suspects needed to contact each week: 300 (G)/48 weeks = 6

While you probably have an awareness of this type of sales pipeline, you may not be referencing it on a regular enough basis. A structured pipeline system like this brings real clarity to your daily activity and literally drives your sales day. There can be no more important function for us in our role as sales professionals than priming the pipeline with an abundance of quality prospects. Yet many only do it when orders dry up and neglect the need when sales are good. As Robert Collier says, 'Success is the sum of small efforts repeated day in and day out', and getting into the habit of prospecting each day through the various methods at your disposal will not only deliver your financial goals, but will develop a mindset and attitude conditioned to success.

> *Repetition is the mother of learning, the father of action, which makes it the architect of accomplishment.*
>
> **Zig Ziglar**

Interestingly, we already have a huge advantage in repeating things as the human mind is programmed to do the same things again and again – we are literally repeating machines. While we could look upon our bad habits as weaknesses, they provide the real-time evidence that we can train our minds to create good habits. Although our brains have many parts, the mind is essentially split into just two: the conscious and the subconscious. Many psychologists claim that up to 98% of the decisions we make each day are driven by the subconscious. In short, we are performing almost everything we do on autopilot.

If at times while reading you have drifted off to reflect on other subject matter, that's your subconscious mind at work. Can you remember when you first learnt to drive a car? During those early lessons, because you hadn't mastered the controls and there was so much going on at the same time, everything you did was very conscious – foot on the clutch, into first gear, release the clutch while pressing the accelerator… It was a real challenge, not made any easier by the instructor next to you shouting insane instructions and playing footsie with the dual controls. However, now you've taken all that constructive and helpful advice and repeated it thousands of times since (assuming you've been driving for more than a year), you can drive a car for long periods of time subconsciously. Similarly, you can create a huge advantage for yourself if you are willing to commit to mastering your sales psychology.

Right now, you and your sales performance sit somewhere within these four areas:

Unconsciously incompetent. Don't take it personally, but you're poor at selling and you simply don't know it.

Consciously incompetent. There's progress. You're still poor at selling, but at least you now know it.

Consciously competent. Now things are cooking. You're good at selling, but you have to focus and practise to make it happen.

Unconsciously competent. Bingo! You're really good at selling and you do it repetitively every day without even thinking.

A bit like a pro golfer who's hit a million balls on the driving range and perfected his swing to the extent where he hardly even needs to think about it, when you are willing to invest the time required to practise and repeat effective sales behaviour, you will achieve the accolade of being unconsciously competent. Psychologists suggest that it takes sixty days to make a habit; just imagine what helpful and constructive sales habits you could have created two months from now. Consider the benefits that new productive behaviour will bring you and your organisation if you're willing to invest in yourself.

Like many prolific sales gurus, Peter Thomson has a lead generation system which is metronomic, consistent and repetitive, and places the written word at its heart. He strongly advocates the need to have something to increase credibility, position yourself as an expert, and in doing so, distance yourself from your competition and collect their share of the business. If you provide your prospect with enough value, and if the 'free gold' that you are offering them is just that – free, then in time the prospect will gain confidence in the sales person – you – and welcome being sold to. A repetitive process of targeted email marketing can become a most effective lead generation system which can literally fill your pipeline to the brim if done respectfully.

There's a real art and science behind the process of generating leads via email. You can research various methods of writing in a way which will give you the best chance of success, but the key defining factor is not too many and not too quickly.

As Peter once told me, 'Ninety per cent of the time you're giving away free gold so that 10% of the time they trust you enough to buy something.' You have to earn the right to convert, and building trust and confidence over the correct amount of time will create a loyal customer. They will not only buy from you, like I did from Peter, but also tell others about you, like I have done in this chapter for Peter.

STICKING POINTS

- **Build your sales pipeline and make it part of your daily focus regime**. Start your day knowing how many calls you need to make to hit and exceed your year-end target – it is a great way to motivate yourself into action.

- **Decide what activity works best for you to create and operate a systematic lead generation system.**

- **Make a list of three things you can incorporate into your lead generation system to position you as an expert in your chosen field.** Then go and make them happen.

Chapter Five

Ready, Aim, Fire!

I used to work alongside a sales guy who was, dare I say it, a little bit old school. By this, I mean he was an absolute gentleman with the ladies, a total lad with the fellas and could hold court at the bar, keeping everyone topped up with suds and stories until the cows came home. If you needed to send in someone to pacify an irate customer, or look after a customer at Ascot races, he was your man, but ask him to confirm who his top fifteen prospects were and at what phase of the sales process they were and he'd struggle. His idea of prospecting was to get out his trusty pin and phone book and start dialling randomly.

While his approach to 'keep smiling and keep dialling' seemed to work for him, I always struggled with his 'every no is one step closer to a yes' mantra. Some of the greatest virtual mentors, like Darren Hardy, author of best-seller *The Compound Effect*, suggest that going after the Nos is the best way to get a yes. Well, that might work for Darren, but it goes against my need to do everything I can to help people make a decision that is good for them.

Just imagine what it feels like after you've secured your eighth straight no of the day. You'll probably be thinking that the ninth isn't far away, given that your self-confidence and inner belief system will have packed their bags and left. The Thinking Cycle has such a massive impact on your outcomes in life, there's a distinct possibility that each no could be creating the negative behaviour that will guarantee the next one follows.

Clearly prospecting brings 'No's, I get that, but the art of sales is always to strive for a 'Yes'. Your time is too precious to waste on nos. A positive response is evidence of great sales behaviour, and with it comes an increased confidence as you know that what you are doing is working. What follows is a massive shot in the arm for your self-belief and the desire to experience more of the same. You will stand tall, you will walk with conviction you'll smile more and, as we know, happy people sell.

To get this level of sales success, start by getting super-focused on your target customer. While the phone book has 1,000 would be customers in it, right now you haven't a clue which ones are suitable and which are not. The only way to be truly efficient at prospecting and to eliminate as many nos as you can is to identify which prospects look like they will buy what you sell. This process is easier than you think, but it requires logic. Fundamentally, ask yourself one basic question: 'Why would people buy the product and service that I have?'

In answering this, you will have started the process of describing your target customer. While this is essential in your quest towards being successful at selling, it's probably not enough for you to start engaging with them just yet. If we use the example of sales training, we could agree that anyone dedicated to a career in sales would want to train to improve their skills and increase their chances of selling more. But if you specialise in training Senior Sales Managers, Sales Directors and Key Account Managers in advanced negotiation and influencing techniques, you'd be wasting your time engaging with tele-sales call-centre staff. By drilling to the next level and engaging in social engineering to investigate further, you can become really clear on who your target customers are and where they operate, and when you know this, you can spend time getting to know more about them before you engage.

Filtering out those who are not aligned with what you offer sounds obvious, yet many sales people don't do it as a matter of procedure every day. Imagine how much time you could create for yourself if you became ultra-disciplined at seeking out only those who are likely to buy from you rather than giving away precious minutes looking at everyone without an end product. The benefit isn't simply to reduce the nos, although that is worth doing; the real benefits come when you are so clear on who will buy from you that you see perfect target customers more and more frequently.

There's a psychological reason why this happens. Part of your brain, called the Reticular Activating System, filters out the masses of data that you are bombarded with every day and allows you to see more of what's important. You tell it what's important by focusing on certain things and consciously thinking about them more often. For example, when someone buys a new car, for days after they've made their selection, all they see is the same make, model and colour car everywhere. Beforehand they didn't notice any, and now they can't stop living in what appears to be some elaborate marketing stunt created by the manufacturer.

It's the same in sales. When you get really focused on your target customer, you will see more of them, and you will see them more often. Your brain will filter out those customers who don't match and refill the head-space with those who do – it's genius, logical and totally natural. With a little practice, you can train yourself to make it happen consistently.

The benefits of being target customer orientated are obvious: a prospect aligned to what you sell suggests more opportunities to do just that; they will probably know similar prospects who could become referrals; you'll be spending your time where the value is rather than working down the page with your pin. Need I go on?

If you chase two rabbits, you catch none.

Chinese proverb

Before we close this chapter, let's look briefly look at the R word – rejection. Because there will always be prospects who, for very valid reasons, decide against benefitting from what we have to offer, we will from time to time encounter a no. Rejection is that feeling when a customer refuses to return our call or reply to our email or gives an objection to our proposal. The Thinking Cycle allows you to recognise the basic principle here: that rejection is a feeling, an emotion. This feeling is created by how we think about what the customer has just done – or, in this case, not done.

It's worth considering the importance of this point in terms of what mastering your psychology can do for your confidence and self-belief – no one can ever make you feel rejected again. Rejection is not something that happens to us; it's created by the way we think. That's massive, isn't it? Especially when you link it to your current sales knowledge and skills together with your appetite to improve your learning to become a true sales expert.

SW3. Some will, some won't, so what, NEXT!

Peter Thomson

Here are some useful practical strategies that you can adopt during every call or meeting to mitigate the chances of ever experiencing rejection in the first place:

Have a minimum of three objectives for every call. Most sales professionals will prepare in advance for every sales call. This technique is one I've used for years specifically to support prospecting. If it's a warm call, and by that I mean the prospect has agreed to take my phone call, objective one would be to get some answers to a few relevant questions to help qualify their suitability. Objective two might be to agree the date and time of the next call to respond to the questions that need more investigating. Objective three might be to get the full explanation of their buying process or permission to add them to my CRM for marketing emails.

Irrespective of what you select as your objectives, the strategy here is to ensure you get something in return for your efforts. Chances are you'll achieve all three, but let's be honest, a rejection of your first objective would emotionally challenge all but the most poker-faced buyer not to agree to the second or third on your list – it's human nature, so this strategy pretty much guarantees you'll get something from every call.

If you've followed the strategy, done everything right, been truly professional in your approach and still got nothing, head for the door and celebrate that you don't need to waste any more of your valuable time on someone who clearly wasn't a target customer after all.

Improve how you use the phone. There are some words to avoid when talking on the phone to prospects. Research suggests that the first seven seconds are critical to whether the buyer decides to progress with the call, so it's worth avoiding the following:

- **'I'm just calling to... '** sounds weak and diminishes what follows. Drop 'just' and be politely assertive when you state the reason for your call.

- **'Can you help me?'** It's not their job to help you, it's your job to help them. Flip it to 'I'd like to ask some questions to see if I can help you... '

- **'Is now a good time to call?'** They were almost certainly doing something and you've just interrupted them, so probably not. Try 'I'm calling to find a good date and time to call you back. I would like to ask you a few questions to see if I can help you... '

- **'If I can show you a way to save X, would you Y?'** Way too early to ask for a decision, it can make you sound like a real sleaze-ball.

- **'I'm calling to see if you got my brochure/proposal/quotation'** – often referred to as the postman approach. It's worth avoiding if you want to maintain integrity.

- **'Just checking in'** – the ASBO approach. Please, don't do it.

Rejection is actually a myth. That there are only three outcomes for every call we make to a prospect – we get a sale, we get a fixed date in the diary following a request for more information or to progress things, or we get a no – suggests that rejection doesn't apply. The no is good news, provided we have followed the steps of the sale sequence correctly and done everything in our power to help the prospect make a decision. We are, after all, in the decision-making business, and we can now devote time to the next prospect.

There are over 7billion people on planet earth, and while most won't be your target customer, some will be. Use the time a no creates for you to go and find a yes.

STICKING POINTS

- **Describe your target customer and use social engineering techniques to learn as much as you can about them to refine your search.** Find out where they go and join them there.

- **Pinpoint the words and phrases that increase your chances of rejection on the phone.** Then remove them from your sales vocabulary.

- **Create a list of your three most important objectives for every call and meeting.** Measure the success rate over a thirty day period to see which ones bring you the best return and use them more often.

Chapter Six

Rapport-building on Steroids

There are a handful of absolute musts that I've incorporated into my daily sales routine. While I'm relieved that I've finally established what these are, I'm somewhat frustrated that I didn't get my head around probably the most important one until much later in my sales career. If you're an experienced Sales Professional, a Sales Manager or Sales Director you will no doubt be all over this key quality, but if you are less experienced and using this book to add value to your sales activity, adopt the tips in this chapter and your relationships with your customers, colleagues and friends will blossom.

In 2008 I was at a social event in the village where I used to live. Typically, about seventy residents would meet four times a year to enjoy each other's company, a glass of wine or

SALES GLUE - THE VITAL INGREDIENT THAT MAKES SALES SUCCESS STICK

two and celebrate the value of close-knit village life. Having organised a few Christmas variety nights and being an active member of the village association, I had become the unofficial entertainments manager, a title that I was happy to look after, being sociable and not shy of the limelight.

Sitting at my table was a couple who had recently moved into the village, and it wasn't long before we struck up a conversation about how much they were enjoying living there. A phrase we hear all the time in sales is 'building rapport', and as a reasonably experienced sales guy I proceeded to do this with the couple, searching for interesting topics to introduce to the conversation in the hope of building a connection. As it often does, the subject quickly moved on to football – bingo! My specialist subject. I have played a bit, I've coached a bit, and as a season ticket holder at Norwich City, I was virtually an expert on the highs and lows of our national game.

What followed was something that, at the time, made a big impact on me and, without me realising the whole significance then, ultimately shaped my life in later years.

As with most of my conversations in those days, I was holding court, giving the couple my take on things because I was good at talking. In fact, I was good at filling a silence – well, someone had to, didn't they? At least, that's what I thought in those days. As the conversation progressed, I pointed out where I thought the professional game was going wrong in terms of players' salaries and how certain players didn't deliver on the big stage while my new friends smiled and listened. I then moved on to the subject of my beloved team and gave them my take on which players we should buy in the next transfer window, which ones we should keep and which we should ban from ever wearing the shirt again. At that point, the husband, Gavin, uttered a set of words which has now become one of the most used phrases in my sales vocabulary.

'What makes you say that?' he said politely, looking genuinely interested.

I continued to force my various footballing opinions on him, and when I allowed him to speak next, he simply replied, 'Really? How do you feel when that happens?'

Over the next ten minutes, he asked me more and more questions about my passion for football, helping me rationalise some of my less than educated assumptions about certain players, allowing me to understand a different point of view and, if I'm honest, giving me clarity on what was worth caring about and what I should let go. Everything we'd spoken about in the last hour was about me and it made me feel good. I enjoyed being listened to, and it was great to share some frustrations and find a solution to make my life, at least the football part of it, a little bit easier and more enjoyable.

"I'm not being funny but I've got 76 slides to get through here and you interrupting and asking questions ain't helping either of us!"

So, feeling quite happy about myself, I thought I'd ask Gavin what he did for a living. 'I'm a Performance Improvement Specialist,' he replied. 'I work with all sorts of people in business and sport, including professional football players, helping them with their psychology, mindset and attitude.'

He'd got my attention.

'When you fully understand what people are like, what challenges they are facing and the pressure they are under, you can establish what sort of support they need to help them improve – whether they're a CEO, a player at Norwich City or a sales professional like you.'

He'd *really* got my attention.

'By making the effort to be interested in them, asking them relevant questions and genuinely listening, we can not only help them, but also benefit ourselves.'

I kept listening and nodding.

'All of my success comes from helping others to solve a problem or improve an area of their performance.'

And right there, in that village hall in a sleepy part of rural England, his words resonated with me. Building rapport, while essential, brought little or no value without the addition of empathy. Gavin had found out a lot about me by asking the right questions, listening to my answer with interest then asking another question based on that answer, yet I knew next to nothing about him, despite having had an equal opportunity that evening to get to know him.

Building rapport is very important in the early part of the sales sequence if we are to build a relationship with the prospect, yet rapport is often described by sales people as 'finding something to talk about for twenty minutes before we get on to selling'. Some even brag about the length of time they can carry on a conversation without getting on to the primary reason why they're in the buyer's office. Poor sales people, poor buyers and a poor waste of time.

Empathy can be defined in a number of ways, but 'putting yourself in another person's shoes' is perhaps the best. Our ability to understand other people is fundamental to success not only in sales, but also in our relationships with our loved ones and friends. It's a quality that I practise daily, often challenging myself to take on another person's point of view and understand it before passing my own judgement.

Stephen Covey's best-selling book *The 7 Habits of Highly Effective People* beautifully defines the skill of empathy:

> ### *Seek first to understand before being understood.*
>
> **Stephen Covey**

Throughout my early years in sales, I was too keen to get a meeting or produce the deck of slides to show the prospect what my company did and how my product differed from the competition. Looking back, I didn't usually get lucky, and it's no wonder. Without knowing the most important factor – the problem they needed solving – I was always playing a game of chance, and that is not how the best sales professionals operate.

One great habit to get into is to approach every interaction with prospects with the objective of getting 'the next click'. This will force you into adopting a more empathetic approach to your selling technique.

Think about want happens when you receive good marketing emails – the ones where real thought has gone into creating value or intrigue; the ones that encourage you to click on a link to a website or download free advice on offer. They are all attempting to do one thing: get the next click.

Regardless of how interesting the email is, we are probably not going to buy whatever is on offer until we've spent more time investigating it. The same is true for those we approach – we have to build value, make it all about them, then ask them to take one small step to move the process forward, building trust and confidence as we go.

Have a look back in your archive to emails you have sent to prospects and print a few. Then take a highlighter pen and highlight everything that describes value for the recipient – i.e. something that solves a problem or the prospect benefits as a result of your message. You might be surprised at how little there is to highlight.

If an email or phone call contains a call to action, for example to phone you back or reply to your email request, then there has to be something in it for the prospect or they probably won't do it. By putting yourself in their shoes, understanding what they want and demonstrating genuine empathy, you ensure that every communication you send has a good chance of getting the other person to click.

As a social species, we have a need to be understood. Think about a time in the last twelve months when, for whatever reason, the person you were in discussion with was adamant that they were right and you were wrong. It probably felt frustrating, and perhaps some negative emotions came into play.

It's possible that you have worked with someone who always had to be right. Often they'd get things done, but their colleagues didn't always do what they wanted with good grace simply because they insisted on criticising people who didn't do things exactly as they would have done. Over time, staff would risk losing their creativity because it was easier to deliver what was asked rather than find other solutions.

The constant need to be right spoils the quality of so many relationships. While I'm not suggesting we have to agree with everyone, everyone has an opinion, and there are real benefits to letting other people make theirs heard, especially in the sales arena.

The lesson I learnt from Gavin back in 2008 paid off for both of us as we went on to become great friends and run a company together. Being empathetic continues to be one of my must dos every day in my sales role because there's so much value in it for me. My challenge to you is to do likewise. Learn to excel at this skill, and as the quality of your relationships grows, so will your sales.

To close this chapter, I want to give you some helpful tips from another of my virtual mentors, Phil Jones. He's a successful speaker who is passionate about helping sales and marketing people improve their skills, and one of the useful things I've learnt from him is to substitute unhelpful words with ones that can help me sell more. I see this skill as a way of helping people come to a decision, which is, after all, what our role in selling is all about.

Replace 'if' with 'when'. 'If' creates a question. When used in a sales context, it presents something that's conditional and therefore needs to be considered. For example, say, 'If you decide to go ahead with our offer', and people will picture the scenario in their mind and reference it against not going ahead with the offer. Substituting 'when' moves the statement from future and conditional to present and active: 'When you decide to go ahead with our offer, you will benefit from this range of extras'. This dramatically increases your chances of success.

Substitute 'we' with 'you'. 'We' is so over-used in sales literature, presentations and pitches. 'We' means we are talking about our own interests, and our prospects and customers, as nice as they may be, have no interest in us at all. They only care about what's in the sale for them. Moving from 'we' to 'you' shifts the conversation over to them: 'Choose us and you will benefit from…', creating value for them and making them more likely to take your offer on board, and that's where the sale happens.

Replace 'expensive' with 'premium option'. 'Expensive' often crops up as an objection and it can kill a sales discussion in a heartbeat if we aren't able to respond to it correctly. Let's face it, everything seems expensive without something to compare it with – at £45,000 a BMW M3 is expensive, except when compared to a Ferrari. Responding to 'it's too expensive' with 'strangely enough, people love to pick the premium option' handles the complaint in a credible way and provides the buyer with more information from which to make the right choice.

Will these three tips guarantee you a sale every time? Possibly not, but they do help eliminate the negative effect that some words have on your conversion rate. So much of your success comes down to what you say, when you say it and how you say it. Adopt these tips and I believe that you will make more of your conversations count.

STICKING POINTS

- **Look to understand your buyer's point of view in every sales discussion.** Make a list of the three main things you believe he/she will want from you and include these in your sales discussions.

- **Adopt an attitude of getting the next click.** It will position your prospect's needs first, help you appear less pushy and make sure you think about building value into every piece of communication you send. There has to be value for the other person if they are to do anything.

- **Eliminate 'if', 'we' and 'expensive' from your sales vocabulary.** Replace them whenever you can with 'when', 'you' and 'premium option'.

Chapter Seven

Walking the Talk

It is commonly accepted that people make a judgement about someone by looking at how they behave. Some say that people make up their minds about you within the first ninety seconds of meeting you for the first time. Take a look at body language expert Mark Bowden's TED Talk entitled 'The Importance of Being Inauthentic'. In his talk, Mark helps us understand that there's a part of our brain that makes snap judgements and, as a result, we psychologically position newcomers in one of four boxes:

Friend. Can this person help me? Will they be kind and bring me value which will improve my standing in some way?

Enemy. Is this person a threat, a predator? Will they rob me of my time or money and bring harm to me or those I care about?

Sexual partner. Is this person good for me? Are we compatible? Can we pair up and produce offspring?

Indifferent. I have no interest in this person, so I won't waste any time on them.

Mark explains that our brain is pre-programmed to adopt the indifferent mode with everyone we meet for the first time. With so much in sales hinging on our ability to create a friend-type of relationship to maximise our chances of success, it's fascinating to know we have far more control over how we can shape this outcome than we might think. Creating a good account of ourselves and the organisation we represent has to be a good strategy to develop. While that may sound simple, I'm amazed at the number of sales people who neglect the fundamentals of their own self-management.

There are obvious practical things we can do, such as having a clean car, good quality clothing, polished shoes, a decent pen and always having a business card to hand. Take a look at the journal you write your notes in, the laptop you share your slides on or the briefcase that you carry – do they all scream, 'I'm a professional person you want to be doing business with'? Successful sales professionals know that each of these tools is as important as the words that they use when they are with clients or prospects. I accept that being authentic is more important than the clothes you wear to a meeting – 'being you' is fundamental. However, if we

˖ ↑ ∩ur prospect to concentrate on the value of what we

say, not what we look like, why risk the outcome by creating a visible distraction?

There are certain people who have a real presence about them. When they walk into a room, they command attention. That doesn't just happen – they earn it. It's a quality that comes with taking real care and attention over their attire and body language. They know that 90% of a person's mind is influenced by what that person sees, with just 10% influenced by what he or she hears.

Given that ratio, why not become a master of controlling the controllable? Pay real attention to who makes your clothes as they might just be a significant factor in how you influence your next prospect. How does it feel when you walk into a room looking good? It feels great. Your shoulders naturally go back, you grow an inch in height and your stride is assertive and long. It does wonders for your confidence and self-belief, and your belief is what defines you.

Everyone's head is full of beliefs. We've all got the world according to us in our own mental satnav system. Your version is different to everyone else's, and as a result, what you are accepting as true or real is different to them. What others believe about you is beyond your total control, although you can influence it somewhat with your appearance and behaviour. But what you believe about yourself is a totally different issue altogether. Quite simply, what you believe about yourself can both increase and limit your performance.

Take five minutes now to write your three responses to this statement:

I'm the sort of sales person who...

- _____
- _____
- _____

Chances are you will have written positive and complimentary things about yourself and your sales ability, such as:

I'm the sort of sales person who:
- Works hard to sell in sequence and learns from mistakes
- Pays attention to customers' needs at all times
- Always follows up every sales opportunity.

Even if you didn't write them down, there may well have been a couple of less than positive things that popped into your head. Here are examples from when I completed the exercise in 2008:

I'm the kind of sales person who:
- Thinks that earning double my current salary isn't achievable
- Doesn't remember people's names very well
- Struggles to handle objections.

Your beliefs are so powerful; they can build you up or knock you down. They act like a thermostat – if the thermostat is set at 19 degrees and the temperature in the room falls below that mark, it kicks into action, firing up the boiler and pumping hot water around the central heating system. Once the temperature reaches 19 degrees, the thermostat shuts down.

In the same way, our inner belief operates like our own mental thermostat, regulating what we do between the performance limits of what we believe we are and are not capable of. We achieve as much or as little as we believe is normal, and as a result, our sales success is being governed by this every day.

My questions to you right now are these: will your belief system allow you to get the most out of life? What's your normal? Do you know how to raise it?

> ***There are millions of people who believe themselves 'doomed' to poverty and failure, because of some strange force over which they have no control. They are the creators of their own 'misfortunes' because of this negative belief, which is picked up by the subconscious mind and translated into its physical equivalent.***
>
> **From *Think and Grow Rich* by Napoleon Hill**

We are all self-limiting; we cannot outperform the boundaries that we set for ourselves. As the quote from the book *Think and Grow Rich* states, so many sales people really do believe they are destined for an average life. They believe that high achievement is outside their control, but really it is they who have created this belief and made it a habit.

As we discussed earlier in this book, our subconscious minds are literally running our lives, with as many as 98% of the decisions we make each day being based on how we have taught our minds to act over our lifetimes. The more we reinforce what we believe we are and are not capable of, the more our subconscious acts on that reality.

We create beliefs in a number of ways, firstly as a consequence of an emotionally intense experience. Phobias and fears are often a result of a childhood experience – for example, a meeting with an aggressive dog or falling into a swimming pool before we learnt to swim. Beliefs manifest as a consequence of adopting someone else's views. Parents and teachers have a significant say in this as we grow up, and quite often youngsters follow their parents' political beliefs when they are old enough to vote.

Later in life, beliefs are created by repetition – repeatedly being told something by others around us or the voice in our head. Self-talk can help or hinder us in our pursuit of sales success. According to Dr Shad Helmstetter, the international best-selling author of sixteen books in the field of personal growth, including *What to Say When You Talk to Yourself*, for as much as 70% of our waking day, we are indulging in self-talk. By the way, just in case you are wondering whether you really have a voice in your head, it's the voice in your head asking you if you have a voice in your head!

Given that you talk to yourself so much, it's crucial that you make the conversation positive, constructive and supportive of your ability to create and achieve your sales goals. One of the most effective ways to tap into constructive self-talk is through affirmations. An affirmation is defined as 'a consciously constructed positive statement written about yourself in the present tense'.

Think about an unhelpful habit you want to break or an area of your sales life you want to improve, take a card or add an entry to the notes section on your phone and write a statement describing how you would behave if the issue had been corrected. In short, remind yourself how you want to be.

Here's an affirmation I've had since 2008:

> **I always shut up and listen with genuine interest when people decide to spend their precious time talking to me.**

By starting your affirmation with positive language such as 'I always…', 'I am… ' or 'I have… ' and committing to reading it every day for two minutes first thing in the morning and two minutes before you retire to bed, you move the words from your conscious mind to your subconscious mind. In doing so, you create a habit via repetition. I've read that affirmation over 6,000 times since I first created it, and now it's no surprise to me that I shut up when people talk to me. Not only that, I really focus on what they are saying, listening to their words and seeking to understand their point of view. I've taught myself to become genuinely interested in them. Think of the benefits that brings me when I'm in front of a prospect for the first time.

You can train your brain in exactly the same way that you would train your abs if you wanted a six-pack. The more you repeat the exercise, the more your brain responds positively. Constructive and helpful thought in delivers constructive and helpful activity out.

There is plenty of research to support the notion that it takes approximately sixty days to make a habit. Read every day, twice a day, for two months, your affirmations will correct the sales faults or limiting beliefs you currently have. The resultant behavioural change will raise your normal and progress you towards sales success.

STICKING POINTS

- **Take more control of how you come across in the first ninety seconds of every new encounter.** Invest in your attire, and create and practise an interest-grabbing opening line that will position you as a friend.

- **Make an honest list of the beliefs you have about yourself that are holding you back.** Decide what action you need to take to improve them.

- **Create three affirmations to correct any bad sales habits you have.** Starting your morning by reading your affirmations will set you up for a really productive day.

Chapter Eight

Objection Overruled!

The topic of how to handle objections is often near the top of a sales person's list of areas to improve. It certainly used to be the case for me.

Handling objections is the part of the process sales people fear, buyers look forward to and sales trainers love – mainly because it's always requested as a must have by the clients they train. There are literally thousands of reference points, videos, posts, audios, podcasts and books available to you right now which will help you to handle the objection. But despite all of those free resources on offer, do you instantly know what to reply when a prospect says, 'It's too expensive'?

I view any and every objection as evidence that I've failed to understand the prospect's needs and pain fully, creating a lack of understanding. A lack of understanding and empathy is likely to stall any relationship from developing and probably subject the sale to a slow and painful death. Objections are also feared by many because, up until they moment they arrive, the sales person has control of the sale. But the instant the prospect objects, the rug is pulled from under the sales person's feet. Now the prospect appears to have control, and whatever the sales person says or does next could make the difference between them staying in the room helping the prospect buy or exiting stage left and getting fired. Talk about pressure!

Objections, and the need to handle them so both we and our prospect can progress through the sales sequence, are a relevant part of the sales process. To understand why they occur, we need to step back and remind ourselves of the key role of the sales professional. Our job is simply this: to help people make a decision that's good for them. All an objection does is halt the decision making process, but the great news is that the prospect still has a problem that needs solving, and we still have the opportunity to solve it.

The three reasons why sales people want training on handling objections are: (a) they don't know how to avoid them, (b) they don't know how to respond when they get them and (c) they get them a lot because of (a) and (b). To every sales person who falls into this category I say, 'Do you really believe in your product? Do you believe that what your product or service offers your customer will help benefit them? Do you value the benefits that your product or service brings so highly that you would buy it yourself?'

> ## *If you are not convinced, you cannot convince.*
>
> **Phil Jones**

If the answer to any of those questions is no then you will find it difficult to handle objections that come your way. Without a firm belief that your customer is going to benefit as a result of what you offer, you impair your ability to help them reach a decision. On the other hand, if the answer to those questions is yes, the combination of your increased belief in yourself (as a result of your psychological learning in earlier pages) and your product or service will serve you well when used with the following advice:

> ## *An objection is not rejection; it is simply a request for more information.*
>
> **Bo Bennett**

Unless the prospect is furious, jumping up and down in front of you and banging a fist on the table – in which case I suggest you accept that you're finished and walk – view the objection as exactly what it is: a request for more information. Apologise and own up to the fact that you didn't provide them with this information at the right time – which is much earlier in the sales sequence during the discover pain part, or 'Suitability' if you're using Ben Chaib's 8S process. Ask more questions here, and the likelihood is that far fewer, or possibly no, objections will follow.

Never disagree when a prospect objects. We've already learnt that human beings have a deep rooted need to be understood, so disagreeing is not going to help you. Notice I haven't suggested you should agree – just accept that they have an opinion. The objective is to diffuse an emotional situation. Diffuse, don't disagree – 3D.

In parallel, mentally check your body language. Find a neutral position, and look the prospect in the eye with slightly raised eyebrows to show you are keen to learn from them. Neither smile nor look serious; the objective is to create an open position to allow them to respond.

With a state of calm now in place, the task moves on to helping the prospect solve their need for more information. To do that, you need them to give you some information first. A great way to progress the objection is to say, 'Why do you say that?' That one simple question, asked with humility and respect, forces the prospect to give you a valid reason why they have an objection. Without a valid reason, they don't have a valid objection.

Before you respond to their feedback, close the sale on everything else. Don't forget, plenty of hard work has already been done between you to get to this point in the sale which can be agreed on and banked. Consider how frustrating it would be if you solved their objection, possibly with a concession, only to find that they drop another objection on the table straight after.

'Other than your concern about price, can we accept that all parts of the proposal are agreed?' or 'If I find a way to solve your issue with the payment terms, is there any reason why you wouldn't then progress to placing an order?' Before you offer any concession, get something in return, and that something is their commitment to move forward.

Finally, prior to conceding commercial ground to get the sale, it's worth moving back into the 'stretch' phase of the sales process. Use a visualisation technique to move the buyer to a virtual place when he/she can imagine what will happen if their problem continues, and the benefit of solving it with your product or service. Maybe this will be all you need to do to handle the objection – it's certainly worth a try.

Commit this to memory to help you when objections arise and you'll find handling them as easy as learning the alphabet:

A – accept the prospect has an opinion. You don't have to agree with it, but right now, they have the control of the sale. That means they have your money.

B – body language that's neutral will remove the threat of emotion. Adopt an open position – sitting up straight with your hands on your knees works best.

C – close on everything else. You've made great progress to get this far, so bank the hard work you've both done.

D – decision before concession. It's time to get an assurance from them that a discount or deal to solve the issue will be worth it.

E – elevate the discussion. Remind them of what they will miss by not going with your solution.

Given that so much sales training is dedicated to handling objections, probably because sales people have experienced most of them in the past, it makes total sense to be aware in advance of what they are so you know the solution before they appear. While specific objections are unique to your own product, service, customer or market, there is one that is common to us all.

Let's build the response which will help solve the prospect's need for further information when they say, 'It costs too much.'

What does the prospect really means when they offer this objection? What is the real source of their concern? It may not be obvious, so this is where the 'Why do you say that?' response is critical. I know from many years of dealing with highly experienced buyers that price, while a factor, is not *the* factor. Far more important to them is that they buy a quality product that doesn't let them down and it arrives on time, every time. They can always buy a cheaper product, but it's their head on the block if their organisation's production fails as a result of them neglecting these two key buying basics.

Quality is enjoyed long after price is forgotten.

Aldo Gucci

So often other factors come into play, and it's key for you to find out the real source of the prospect's objection if you are to address it for them fully and move the discussion forward. 'It costs too much' could mean:

- They don't understand the true value of what you are offering
- They can genuinely buy it more cheaply elsewhere
- They can't afford it.
- They don't want to buy from you.

In order to progress things, respectfully seek a comparison. Without being compared to an alternative, everything looks expensive (or cheap). Let's say your prospect can buy a product 5% cheaper than yours. Here's one possible way you can make progress:

'I understand how you feel. Making an important investment in a premium option like ours needs to be benchmarked. I would do the same in your situation.'

An initial response like this takes a lot of the emotion out of the situation because you've understood the prospect (empathy). Note that you haven't agreed with them, though; you have positioned yourself and your product above the competition by signalling that your difference in price is justified. You may decide to reduce your price, but that's your decision, not theirs. The process of regaining control begins.

'It's worth reflecting on the fact that our product will create real value for your business over its lifetime. You agreed that it is the right solution based on the benefits we discussed earlier.'

Visualising the future helps take the focus away from the short-term issue of price and moves the prospect on to a long-term view of ease. They don't want the hassle that comes with inferior cheaper products. You may decide to remind them now of the cost of inactivity, or possibly the impact of down-time if they do buy a cheaper product – take care with this point, though. Bashing the competition is not something I recommend.

'Given that we've agreed everything other than price, can we also agree that, provided we find a way to bridge the gap, you will go ahead with the order today?'

This is essentially a closing technique that not only gauges how close you are to the actual sale, but also mitigates any chances of the prospect dropping another objection onto the table after you've handled price for them. You've got control.

If you get their agreement, you simply need to decide whether and how to handle their request to reduce your commercial offering. There are many ways you can do this. In my career, discussions of this nature would allow for the customer to receive the concession at the end of a certain period of time or when they had bought an agreed quantity – they get what they want, but on my timescales. This creates a win/win. It's also worth considering the importance of lifetime value when confronting not just price based objections, but all the roadblocks that upset the sales process from playing out successfully.

Rather than thinking about a single sales transaction with a new customer, consider how much income this new customer will bring your organisation over the next five years if you keep them happy. Factor in the potential they have to introduce you to other prospects through referrals and introductions, and you could be looking at significant revenue ahead. If you look at each prospect through this lens and adopt an approach that befits the size of the opportunity, you help them decide to buy more often.

There are clearly many other objections that could crop up. Use them as a barometer to gauge how good you are at understanding the customer's needs. The better you become at this, the fewer objections you will get. They will come though, so plan ahead. Consider the following objections and plan a half-day in your diary to create an ABCDE process to respond to them:

- 'I want time to think about it'
- 'I need to talk it over with others'
- 'I'm happy with my existing supplier'
- 'I'm seeing two other suppliers after you, so will let you know'

- 'Call me back in six months, the time isn't right'
- 'We don't have the budget'.

You could create a spreadsheet and list column A 'Objection', column B 'Reason' and column C 'My response'. Complete each cell in each column and you will have a ready-made search engine to give you instant data whenever you need it. Print it off and keep a copy in your car, reflecting on it every time you hit traffic or before you go into a meeting – make it a habit.

Visualise yourself about to meet with a warm prospect who has already signalled their intent to buy. These tools in your psychological sales tool kit must improve your level of confidence and self-belief about your own ability to help them buy. You also have your three objectives written down to help steer you both towards the joint goal of solving their problem. Add to that your commitment to taking your prospect through the 8S Sales Process, with each step building value and creating clarity for them so they can see that what you have is what they want to buy. The buyer will be nodding in agreement, at ease with you, his/her body language will be relaxed, at times mirroring yours as if to say, 'We're compatible, this feels right'. Nothing has been left to chance. Prepare for every concern and objection your prospect may have and you will be filled with confidence and excitement about the meeting ahead and your unwavering desire to help them make a decision. Isn't that a mindset geared for sales success?

STICKING POINTS

- **An objection is created by you, not the prospect.** Spend more time understanding their pain early in the sales sequence with great questions to reduce objections.

- **Use the ABCDE approach.** When objections come, remember 3D – diffuse, don't disagree.

- **Build a database of possible objections.** Pinpoint the real reason why they come and create an answer for each – learn them, and I promise they will boost your confidence, becoming a great help for both you and your prospect.

Eyes on the Prize

In the last chapter we touched on emotion when we looked at rejection, and earlier in the book we learnt about the very foundation of *Sales Glue*, the Thinking Cycle. I want to build on that learning.

As someone who operates in an area where psychology and the art of selling meet, I'm always looking for science to support why we think the way we do and how that drives what we do. If evidence proves I can think, feel and behave in a certain way, I'm going to buy into that. There is plenty of evidence from the field of psychology to support the theory that what we think about, we get more of, so we can really commit to developing a constructive and productive sales psychology.

We know rejection is an emotion that comes from our thoughts. Given that we have almost total control over how we think, we can genuinely look at rejection as something we create ourselves rather than something that just happens when things don't go our way.

But why don't things go our way all the time in sales? Is it too much to expect things to go right 100% of the time? The answer to that must be yes. Even the very best sales professionals I've studied have experienced bucket loads of rejection in their careers, and still do. Some of the reason is down to the simple fact that not everyone will want what you sell, and even the ones who do may not want it in your timescale. This helps us see that rejection and failure are part of the process.

We have further evidence in the Sales Pipeline exercise in Chapter Four where we factor in failure based on the need to approach a certain number of suspects to find a qualified prospect. There's a calculated number of nos built into that process, so we accept the nos will come.

Quite often, however, rejection comes our way when it shouldn't. We fail to prepare, plan and execute in ways that will mitigate the chances of things going wrong:

- We don't follow the sales system and fail to identify the pain
- We make it all about us, too keen to get on to our slides about our product
- We try to sell and people hate to be sold to

- We look desperate, our pipeline is empty and we become pushy
- We don't put in the effort and our pipeline dries up
- We fail to identify areas where we could improve our skills
- We don't follow up
- We mistake being busy for the productive activity designed to meet our goals
- We don't have any goals.
- We talk too much, we don't listen, we're always right.

So much of this lack of preparation is down to a lack of focus. There are many things all trying to get our attention and disrupt our focus – consider how many times people reach for their phones each day. A study led by Nottingham Trent University discovered that an average person checks their device eighty-five times a day, spending a total of five hours browsing the web and checking apps.

I'm not suggesting we shouldn't do that, but when we look at the fact that we can only ever have one conscious thought at any given time, the phrase 'multi-tasking' is flawed. When we dig into the psychological evidence associated with how we naturally think, the facts show that without realising it, we can think in less than helpful ways, and this could be a reason why so many sales people lack motivation.

> ## *44% of salespeople give up after one follow-up.*
>
> **Scripted**

Imagine that you've been asked to walk along an RSJ steel beam – the kind that you see exposed in office blocks during the build phase. This one is 30mm x 30mm, 25 metres in length, lying on the floor, and at one end I've put a £20 note. Could you walk along the beam without falling off? If you can, the money is yours. Most people would have a go and probably complete this relatively straightforward task.

Now let's imagine the beam is suspended over Oxford Street in London, 100m up in the air between the buildings that line the famous thoroughfare, and the rush hour traffic is passing beneath you. Visualise the £20 note at the far end. Could you repeat the earlier task in this new location and place one foot in front of the other to reach the money? Apart from the odd thrill seeker, pretty much everyone I take through this mental task declines at this point.

While the two tasks described above are identical, the introduction of height, or 'risk' for want of a better description, starts a mental process which is all too frequent for us when faced with problems. The change of location literally shifts our focus away from the banknote to the road 100 metres below, and clearly that's not where we want to go.

Clearly no one visualises themselves on the beam thinking, *I want to fall*, because that would be stupid. What they are actually thinking is, *I don't want to fall*, and that in itself creates a familiar set of chain reactions. They feel nervous, anxious and scared. Those feelings increase their heart rate. They could well be starting to sweat or perspire, their breathing, which was deep and controlled, is now short and intense, and their legs – well, they've just turned to jelly.

The more we fill our thoughts with images of what we don't want to happen, the more we create the emotions and behaviours conducive with making that thing happen. This phenomenon is due to the laser-like teleological nature of the brain which is conditioned to lock on to whatever it is we think about. The human brain is very directional, very outcome orientated, just like a heat-seeking missile attaching itself to the target. Consider again that up to 98% of what we are doing on any average day is driven by the subconscious habits that we've created over time through repetition. Because our subconscious mind has been conditioned by our conscious thought processes and is the source of so much of what we do each day, it is vitally important to put helpful, constructive thoughts in if we are to benefit from productive activity.

While consciously we know the difference, our subconscious finds it difficult to differentiate between something that we want and something that we don't want if we're focusing on it – it's just as likely to lock on to it and do it or take you there.

On top of all of this neural knowledge, here's a weird phrase to burn into your memory: 'The human brain can't do a don't'.

Let me give you an example. Picture yourself in the pub with a group of friends, in a small circle all facing each other. The conversation is lively, there's plenty of laughter, and everyone's enjoying themselves, but all of a sudden, one of your friends looks past you to the pub door.

With a surprised look on their face, they blurt out 'Whatever you do, don't turn around now.' What's the first thing you're likely to do? In that split second, you turn around.

Clear your mind, take a deep breath and focus on the next set of words consciously. For three seconds, try hard not to think of a giraffe.

Did you think of a giraffe?

These are two simple examples of how, when people are told not to do something, they can't help themselves, at least not for the first couple of seconds. This naturally occurring phenomenon can have some pretty dramatic and destructive influences over our ability to keep our sales focus in the right direction.

Consider this: there are many sales people right now who are operating in a difficult economic climate, trying desperately hard not to miss this month's sales targets. You could say they are focusing on *not* failing. Clearly, given the teleological nature of the brain and the fact that it can't do a don't, if they go into a sales situation trying hard not to fail, they can't be surprised if they don't get the outcome they were hoping for.

If you're trying not to miss a sales target, what thoughts will be in your head for a fair amount of your day? Will they be helpful and constructive images of successful prospect appointments, orders flowing into your organisation, inspirational sales team meetings and happy customers? Or will they be something quite different: rejection, desperation and defeat? What feelings do each of those sets of images conjure up in your mind, and what behaviour and activity do they inspire? When you look at it like this, it's very easy to see the massive impact that the Thinking Cycle and your ability to manage it has on your results.

The more we get our focus on to what we want rather than what we don't want, the more we take advantage of the way the brain naturally functions. Focus on the sales behaviours you need to demonstrate; focus on how you want to feel; focus on what you're looking to create for yourself.

> *People often say that motivation doesn't last. Well, neither does bathing - that's why we recommend it daily.*
>
> **Zig Ziglar**

I remember a corporate selling role I once had. Almost every year, my product would come under attack from the competition who had a lower cost price as a result of manufacturing from a different raw material. Each year I would defend my product and renegotiate with my customers to avoid big losses, but inevitably I would see a volume reduction, and the reluctant message from above would be to lower the forecast target. While I believe that everyone in the organisation was doing the best they could in the circumstances, in hindsight our focus had become conditioned on trying not to fail rather than on innovative ways to grow market share, succeed and hit budget.

From today, I encourage you to commit to getting focused on the things that I've shared in the book so far which, if implemented, will bring you the best chance of sales success. Do them consistently in a pragmatic and professional way, and you will experience more of the outcomes you want and limit those you don't want. Recognise that rejection is part of the process; not everyone will buy, so everyone in sales will experience it at some point. Be mindful that you create the feeling of rejection based on how you think. You are in control of your feelings, not the prospect, buyer or customer.

CHAPTER 9 – EYES ON THE PRIZE

STICKING POINTS

- **Control the controllable.** List ten things you can control which, if done well, will limit the chances of you being rejected on a sales call. Identify which you may need to improve upon and take action to do so.

- **Make a list of all the things you do want and don't want in your sales role.** Channel all your focus and energy into activities designed to give you more of what you want.

- **If you feel rejection, take a deep breath and reflect.** Recognise that you can change the feeling by changing the way you think. Learn what's creating that negative emotion and act to stop it happening again.

Chapter Ten

The Close? They Haven't Already Bought?

There used to be a general acceptance that the close was a unique ring-fenced event which took place at the point when the customer was ready to buy. It was designed purely to get them over the line and say yes.

While I cannot deny that this is a fundamental and necessary part of the sales process, I, and many more in the sales training industry, believe that the close doesn't come at the end. It starts at the very beginning of the sales sequence when we earn the prospect's trust and continues throughout the sequence. Do everything I've advised and I believe that the close will, more often than not, happen naturally without the need to use some elaborate closing gymnastics routine. I see the close as simply an endorsement that you have done your job well – you've helped the customer make a decision which is right for them. In fact, you've exceeded their expectations.

While it is your responsibility to close the sale, the bigger responsibility lies in earning the sale. The close is for the customer, not for you – help them make a decision and all you will need to do before they buy is ask for the business. Please make sure you *always* ask for the business. So many sales people don't do this and leave opportunities on the table – don't be that guy or girl.

I have been searching for some classic sales closing techniques and have come up with three that could backfire spectacularly, unless done properly. All three are great ways to gain a final commitment, though, so you can practise them and use them in the right way.

The porcupine close.

The objective: get the prospect to answer their own question with a yes by aligning your question to the one that they've asked. In other words, you throw their question back at them as if they'd thrown you a spiky porcupine (as if!).

Here's how it should go: the prospect asks, 'Does it come in red?' and you reply, 'Would you like it in red?' Ideally, their signal to buy will be reflected in their reply, 'Yes', and you close with, 'Let me get that for you right now'.

Here's how it could go: the prospect looks at you like you're a sleaze-ball and says, 'Who said I was going to buy it?'

The score close.

The objective: the prospect gives you a score out of ten that confirms their interest in your solution. A high score allows you to get them to confirm why they like it.

Here's how it should go: you ask, 'On a scale of one to ten, what score would describe how you feel about our product being right for you?' If the score exceeds seven, ask them, 'Really? Why so high?' and in theory, they will tell you (and themselves) all the reasons why they like it. They're sold.

Here's how it could go: they reply, 'One. It's rubbish.'

The fluffy bunny close.

The objective: the prospect is given your product to try for free for a short time in the hope that they'll fall in love with it like they would with a lovely fluffy bunny.

Here's how it should go: you say, 'Try the car for the weekend. Put it to the test, put some miles on the clock and enjoy yourself. I think you'll love it.' The customer does as you suggest, they do grow to love it, and the guilt of using it and not buying it is too much, so they buy.

Here's what could happen: the customer does what you say and drives 500 miles over the weekend, stopping briefly to arrange a demo offer with a competitor dealer for next weekend before handing you back the keys.

These examples may have resonated with you. While they are a little tongue in cheek, they identify the potential risk that comes with placing too much emphasis on closing someone who isn't totally convinced about what you're offering. Having said that, I hope they have raised your curiosity enough to learn more about different closing tactics and techniques – there are hundreds to choose from.

Without your prospect committing to buy, signing the paperwork or handing over money in exchange for your goods and services, you haven't helped them, and you haven't completed the job. My advice is for you to find a handful of closing techniques that work for you and are conducive to your customer, product and market and make them a habit. In all likelihood you'll never need to use them, given that your energy, focus and activity will already have been devoted to gaining the prospect's trust and commitment to buy much earlier in the selling process.

The close starts at the start, not the finish.

STICKING POINTS

■ Your ability to help your customer commit to buying your product or service will be significantly improved if you've taken them through the four previous steps of the Sales Sequence in Chapter Three. Take a few minutes now to remind yourself of what those four steps are.

■ **Research and find three closing techniques that are relative to your market.** Learn them. Practise them with your sales colleagues in role play scenarios until you've mastered them and can deliver them at the right time to help your prospect commit.

■ **Remember, the close is for them, not you.** You are helping the customer make a decision, so be confident. This is ultimately what they want you to do.

Chapter Eleven

Sales Motivation. How Do You Do You?

I hope that your investment in *Sales Glue* has been a good one and you're feeling motivated, optimistic about your future and inspired to put your new learning into practice. Something has probably been going on inside your head for some time that prompted you to take this action and read *Sales Glue*. Keep going – you're closer than you might think to sales success.

So what is it inside people like us that makes us search out advice and wisdom to improve our sales skills and benefit ourselves? Why doesn't everyone do the same? Statistics suggest that the average person reads only one book per year. Counter that with the fact that 85% of self-made millionaires read two or more books every month. Warren Buffet reads for six hours a day and it's netted him over $60billion. According to *The Business Dictionary*:

> ***Motivation results from the interaction of both conscious and unconscious factors such as the (1) intensity of desire or need, (2) incentive or reward value of the goal, and (3) expectations of the individual and of his or her peers.***

Based on this definition, it's fair to say that so much of what motivates us in sales is born from us wanting to receive a prize, be that in monetary terms, accolade or recognition from others. We want to move towards the things that bring us pleasure – we can call this 'to motivation'. Conversely, the definition could mean the opposite – we have to sell to get paid, and if we don't we're out of a job. We can call this 'away motivation', and we are actiing to get as far away from this outcome as possible because it's painful.

The challenge in both these scenarios is not always obvious, but is so important if we are to become motivated enough to create productive and sustainable sales activity. The problem with 'away motivation' is that while it will quickly get us moving away from a problem, our thought process is likely to be a negative one. If we go back to the huge importance of the Thinking Cycle and its influence over our outcomes, we see that unhelpful thoughts create negative emotions. We don't feel excited about achieving sales to avoid the sack; we'll do it, but we won't enjoy it.

'Away motivation' is not conducive to well thought-through, pragmatic relationship building with prospects, which is the foundation for sales and repeat business. It's likely this will be rushed and we will look and sound desperate.

On the other hand, 'to motivation' works on the premise that the prize in the distance is one worth heading towards and it warrants a sustained plan of action to reach it. While the challenge is to be disciplined to maintain the plan long enough, help is at hand in the shape of our mind and the way it naturally wants to function. We know from Chapter Nine that we have a teleological brain that literally locks on to whatever we focus on. The more we focus on the things we want, saturating our thoughts with the glory of achievement, the more we will gravitate towards it with our daily sales activity and behaviour.

So how do we create a mindset conditioned to long-term habitual productive sales behaviour? Firstly, we establish what the goal is we are aiming to achieve. Sounds obvious, but without a destination, how can we start the journey on the most efficient route?

> ### *If you aim at nothing, you'll hit it every time.*
> **Zig Ziglar**

What does being a sales expert look like? When did you last sit down and benchmark your skillset to understand how satisfied you are? How well are you doing and what could you improve?

The sales audit coming up in this chapter has been created to enable you to establish just that. Look at each area of sales shown on the left hand side of the chart and score how satisfied you feel about each out of ten. If, for example, your LinkedIn profile is up-to-date and really talks to your target audience, then you will probably give that a high score – you're satisfied with that area of your sales life. If this book has reminded you of the lack of time you invest in learning new sales skills, you will possibly score 'Regular Learning' much lower. Shade the box under the number that corresponds with how you feel.

Repeat this process for each of the sales areas until your page is complete. It's really important that you are honest with your scores, so don't over-think each one. Just go with your gut feeling. By doing this exercise you are establishing how satisfied you are about your current level of sales acumen – your 'clear current reality' – which is something that very few sales professionals ever do. So enjoy the experience, knowing that you're already ahead of most in your industry and closer than ever before to creating the strategy that will define and shape your future.

Area of Sales	Satisfaction Score Out of 10									
	1	2	3	4	5	6	7	8	9	10
Networking	☐	☐	☐	☐	☐	☐	☐	☐	☐	☐
Prospecting	☐	☐	☐	☐	☐	☐	☐	☐	☐	☐
Social Engineering	☐	☐	☐	☐	☐	☐	☐	☐	☐	☐
Questioning Skills	☐	☐	☐	☐	☐	☐	☐	☐	☐	☐
Listening	☐	☐	☐	☐	☐	☐	☐	☐	☐	☐
Public Speaking	☐	☐	☐	☐	☐	☐	☐	☐	☐	☐
Handling Objections	☐	☐	☐	☐	☐	☐	☐	☐	☐	☐
Social Media Presence	☐	☐	☐	☐	☐	☐	☐	☐	☐	☐
Product Knowledge	☐	☐	☐	☐	☐	☐	☐	☐	☐	☐
Competitor Knowledge	☐	☐	☐	☐	☐	☐	☐	☐	☐	☐
Receiving Referrals	☐	☐	☐	☐	☐	☐	☐	☐	☐	☐
Attitude & Mindset	☐	☐	☐	☐	☐	☐	☐	☐	☐	☐
Body Language Skills	☐	☐	☐	☐	☐	☐	☐	☐	☐	☐
Regular Learning	☐	☐	☐	☐	☐	☐	☐	☐	☐	☐
Target Market Knowledge	☐	☐	☐	☐	☐	☐	☐	☐	☐	☐

While this exercise is simple by nature and relatively quick to do, don't under-estimate its importance. Provided you've been honest, right there in front of you is your clear current reality of your level of satisfaction about your sales life. It is the result of all your hard work and effort to date, a visual representation of the investment you've made in the skills that you need to be among the best in your field at selling.

How do your scores make you feel right now? Are you excited? Satisfied? Surprised? Concerned? The benefit of your sales audit is that you can take pride and satisfaction from the areas with high scores and choose to act to improve those areas which have lower scores. Improvements in these areas will benefit how you help people buy your products and services, and that tends to come with increased sales and rewards for you. The key thing is you now have real clarity on where to act and can create your clear future reality.

> ## *Begin with the end in mind.*
> **Steven Covey**

Let's take your newfound clear current sales clarity and put it to good use. Select one area of your sales audit where you are less than satisfied with your current score – let's assume it's your Questioning Skills and you've scored yourself six out of ten. My question to you would be: 'What does ten out of ten look like?' Take a piece of paper and a pen and write down all the things you can think of that would describe a ten out of ten.

If we continue with our example of Questioning Skills, to be really great at asking relevant questions specific to your prospect's needs, you'll need to spend quality time researching them. Establish a handful of key questions to use every time you meet that will lead you into the 'stretch' phase of the sales sequence. Your prospect will then be willing and happy to share information with you.

It feels good, doesn't it, writing those words, describing your clear future reality, essentially predicting the future. What you've produced in a relatively short space of time is a piece of your blueprint for sales success. That's pretty damn special. It's also potentially worth a huge amount of money, both for you and your organisation, because if you decide to act on your own advice and create a load of tens, not only will your stock value rise as a result, but your ability to provide a great experience to your prospects and customers will improve.

Ask yourself, 'Is what I've written on that paper achievable?' There may be some resource issues required to deliver it, possibly some investment of cash in training and certainly some investment of time on your part, but we can assume these will deliver a return on investment (they will, trust me), so what's stopping you from taking action?

Ready to make it happen?

STICKING POINTS

- **Complete the sales audit exercise every three months.** To keep moving forward with your progress, measure and plot your improvements.

- **Create a word picture to describe what a ten out of ten looks like for each area of low satisfaction.** Introduce the learning and skills required to turn this picture into reality.

  - **Involve your manager.** Get their buy-in and funding for the training you need. They will then see the return on investment and support your progression.

Chapter Twelve

A Goal Without a Plan Is Just a Wish

I'm passionate about selling, as you can probably tell. Not only is the profession of selling a noble one, but everyone sells. Whether we're talking to our boss about a salary increase, our spouse about where to go on holiday or persuading our kids to brush their teeth at night, we all sell.

I've used goal setting for years and I couldn't image life without it. Every athlete who has represented their country at the Olympic Games will have relied on a goal setting strategy to position themselves at the top of their sport. Yet very few adults set goals, and those who do struggle to maintain them. Why?

"I knew that new-age crap wouldn't work Simkins!"

Like many people, I've set myself a New Year's resolution at some point in my life. I've been standing at a party, drink in my hand and a bit of Dutch courage inside me as I say, 'Yep, the jeans are a bit snug. This year I will lose a bit of weight.' What starts off in the first week of January as a disciplined effort to achieve said goal becomes a bit of a challenge by week two when my new trainers give me blisters after my one and only run. I soldier on into week three, but the moment my friends invite me out for a curry, I opt to trade broccoli smoothies for a chicken madras and six pints of Kingfisher.

The bottom line is this: without the two fundamental qualities required to achieve any goal, we will always struggle. These two qualities, held with enough conviction, will create unstoppable persistence, and they are belief and desire.

On 6 May 1954 at the Iffley Road track in Oxford, UK, Roger Bannister broke the 4 minute mile with a time of 3 minutes 59.4 seconds. That itself was an astonishing feat, especially given that at the time, there was a genuine fear that any human attempting to run that quickly would be in serious danger of long-term physical health issues, possibly even death. Clearly Bannister had huge amounts of belief in his own ability to succeed and a desire so strong he ignored the possible risk to his health. Undeterred, he achieved his goal and rewrote the pages of history for ever.

However, what followed forty-six days later was, in my opinion, an even greater example of how personal psychology can positively impact personal performance. On 21 June in Turku, Finland, the Australian runner John Landy broke Bannister's record with a time of 3 minutes 57.9 seconds. Whatever self-limiting belief Landy may have had previously about humans not being able to break 4 minutes was instantly lifted by Roger Bannister.

> ### *There is nothing that belief plus a burning desire cannot make real.*
>
> **Napoleon Hill**

Goal setting and sales success go hand in hand for me, and you can consider adopting a similar thought process. In the same way that affirmations will help you to correct a poor sales habit, goal setting will help you lock on to and achieve any sales target you set for yourself. Not only that, you can take it into any walk of life and apply it with confidence, knowing that it will deliver results – provided you want to achieve and believe you can.

The process I'm going to share with you is called the Mindspan 4x4 Goal Setting Process. It involves two sets of four components that, when combined, deliver a framework for sales success. Is it simple? Yes. Is it easy? No, but what in life that's worth having is easy to come by? Will it allow you to maintain a disciplined focus way past week three in January? Absolutely.

The first set of four components are as follows:

Write your goal down personally. If the goal is about you, it will start with 'I'. If it's a team goal, it will start with 'we'.

Write your goal down in the present tense. This allows you to picture yourself actually completing the goal. Most goals fail because people cannot picture the benefit. When you see it in your mind, you can go after it physically.

Make sure the outcome is clearly defined. There's a big difference between 'I should lose some weight' and 'I weigh 75kg, which is 15kg less than I did three months ago'. The teleological nature of the brain can lock on to the clarity of that information much more easily than it would to 'lose some weight'.

Write a date of completion. Again, most goals fail because people never get around to finishing them. Putting a date on your goal galvanises you into doing the activity required within the timescale you've set.

Here's a goal of mine that I set in July 2016 before I started to write this book. See how it falls exactly in-line with the first part of the 4x4 process outlined above.

> It's December 2016 and I'm gift-wrapping copies of my new book *Sales Glue* to give to friends and prospects for Christmas. I've received some really positive feedback via Amazon and Twitter, and opportunities to speak in public about my book are increasing.

I looked at that goal twice a day, every day, for three months as I wrote the chapters, agreed on the right cover design and completed the various elements of the publishing process. The fact that I pictured myself wrapping copies to give as Christmas presents and committed to growing my business off the back of the achievement created an immense amount of belief that I could do it and a real desire to succeed.

Now it's your turn. Refer to the work you did in the previous chapter and the word picture you created to illustrate a ten out of ten, and create a goal using the written part of the 4x4 method. Don't worry if it takes a few attempts to get it right, just make sure you follow the four steps exactly and you will get there. Repeat the process with two or three more goals from the less than satisfactory areas of your sales audit until you have a number of sales goals that both inspire and excite you into action. Don't overdo it, mind. Too many goals and you won't give yourself enough time to complete the relevant activity. On the flip side, too few and you'll find yourself focusing all your time on one area, and that could negatively impact other important tasks and duties within your sales role. It's all about balance.

Writing goals this way is a relatively simple process. But like a car won't go anywhere without a tankful of fuel, you now need to bring your goals to life and move them forward. You do this by 'emotionalising' them.

The second set of four components relies on you using sales psychology. Adopt:

Positive self-talk. When you look at your goal first thing in the morning and last thing at night, the voice in your head will read it to you. It's crucial that you make this self-talk constructive. Say the goal like you mean it, with purpose and conviction.

Regular positive visualisation. Because your subconscious mind cannot tell the difference between something that's real and something that you imagine, allow your brain to believe the goal is actually happening and that is so powerful for the following two points.

Strong positive belief. If you see yourself achieving the goal and enjoying the benefits that come with completing it, you will naturally raise you level of self-belief, keeping you on task to execute the workload.

A genuine desire to achieve. The more you read the goal, see yourself achieving it and enjoying the fruits of your hard work, the more you will want it.

So there you have it: a proven framework that, provided you read your goals twice a day for two minutes at a time, will guarantee you the best possible chance of achieving your targets on your journey towards sales success.

> ### *If you can dream it, you can do it.*
> **Walt Disney**

The final, and possibly the most important, part of setting and achieving a goal this way is to recognise it must never be left until you've taken the first step. What is the first thing you need to do to set the goal in motion? For me, it was to come up with the titles of the chapters and write five bullet points to describe the content of each chapter. Once I had these written down and could see the framework of the book in front of me, I was sold.

What will your first step be to start the journey to achieving your goals? Take some time away from the book right now, write your goals out, define your first action and get ready to achieve greatness.

STICKING POINTS

- **Set yourself three sales goals and three personal goals.** Write them down and adopt the daily 4x4 goal setting method.

- **Sit down with your sales team.** Share the 4x4 method and create some team goals that will define the success of your company over the next twelve months.

- Keep your goals close to hand so you can review them daily —on your notes section of your phone, stuck on your bathroom mirror or on cards in your briefcase.

Chapter Thirteen

The Attitude of Gratitude

'Value' is a word we hear a lot in sales. You probably say it a lot yourself. It goes without saying that the more you establish what value your prospect is looking for and link that to the value you can demonstrate in your product and service, the more successful you will be.

There is a danger, however, that the word 'value' is starting to become a bit overused. It gets bandied about all over the place and is as synonymous with sales as 'coffee is for closers' was back in the nineties. Of course value is important and always will be, but if you use it in a slightly different way, it will create greater impact on your sales success. Don't just *add* value, *give* it, and give it in bucket loads. Give it even when you don't expect to get anything in return.

Yes, you heard me right. Find as much value as is within your personal control and give it to the people who have an influence in your life, be that your sales life or your personal life. So much of what you have achieved so far has come as a direct result of how you have influenced people. For example, if you're considering going for a bigger sales role, perhaps with greater responsibility, remember you're not in that role yet for a reason. Possibly it is because you haven't influenced people enough, because if you had you'd be doing that job already. Consider for a minute how many people you've had to gain cooperation from this week in order to get something in return. Your spouse, kids, boss, taxi driver – the list is endless.

To gain cooperation, we need to influence people. If we want to exceed our sales quota, we have to influence our customers to buy from us. If we want to fill our pipeline, we have to influence prospects, convincing them that what we have is important enough for them to allow a discussion to take place. If we want a better job, we have to influence our organisation or the recruitment people to move us there.

Here's a quick visualisation exercise for you. Think of one person in your life, not including a close family member, who would drop everything and be there if you needed their help. Got their picture in your head? Now think of somebody who wouldn't lift a finger, instead giving you a reason (objection) as to why they couldn't help you. Why is there is a difference between the two scenarios? How have you influenced the first person so greatly that they would always have your back? What did you do? It must have been something special. Think about the benefits that come with a relationship where you have earned the right to invade a person's life and get their instant cooperation and help. If they'd do so much without warning, my guess is they'd do even more with prior notification. Interesting.

Equally important is the fact that you have someone in your network whom you can't influence in the same way. But before you consider deleting them from your friends list, learn why you can't get their help and correct whatever the reason is. Wouldn't it be useful to have their cooperation in the future? Maybe you can think of a prospect, customer or buyer who fits into this category. You can never get hold of them; they don't return your calls or emails; it's difficult to build rapport. But you still want them to buy from you, don't you?

There's a reason why the first person will do practically anything for you – they like you. They like you because you have consistently taken an interest in them over a sustained period of time, and they like the fact that you are interested in them. Everyone you meet, you open up an 'emotional bank account' with. Depending on the level of investment you make into that account, how you engage with the person and the interest you take in them, you will be either in credit or debit. And as important is the fact that everyone you meet opens up an emotional bank account with you.

You can almost certainly come up with a long list of examples of how you've invested in the first person you thought of. You listen to them with genuine interest and don't interrupt; you allow them to air their opinion; you spend time with them; you buy them gifts, and not only on special occasions. Put simply, you make regular investments to keep their emotional bank account topped up so that when you need to make a withdrawal, you are always in credit.

Now think of the second person. You probably haven't done any of the things you've done for the first person, and as a result, you're out of credit. It's exactly the same with customer relationships. If you put aside how you interact with prospects and focus simply on existing customers, how many do you have right now who would drop everything and help you out? These are people who already buy from you. They are convinced that what you offer will solve their problem, and quite possibly have the ability to give you more business, and take business away from you too. Chances are you've invested heavily in their emotional bank account. Have a think about what you are currently doing to influence your customers in ways that will reinforce the reasons why they buy from you. What are you doing with them to help them buy more from you – and find you new business? It's sales nirvana when your existing customers become your lead generation system.

You've already discovered over thirty proven practical tips in *Sales Glue* specifically designed to help you become a highly-motivated, high-performing sales expert, so surely it would be wrong to miss leveraging this potential additional business that most sales people don't benefit from. For the output of your customer relationships to be their cooperation in helping you in some way, then the input must be your genuine desire to invest in that relationship. We need fewer than twelve key relationships in life to get to the heights of success, so go and find them, cultivate goodwill, demonstrate genuine empathy, invest in them and see what happens.

> ## *You can have everything in life you want if you'll just help enough other people get what they want.*
>
> **Zig Ziglar**

Here are a few ideas and strategies that have served me well over the years. I encourage you to introduce them into your own sales approach:

Call your top twenty-five customers today and thank them for their business. Some people might feel worried this will inject suspicion into the customers' minds, and I get that. I used to think the same way until I realised that such a conversation is a barometer to measure what my customers think of me and my organisation. Call yours and say thank you. If it provokes a sarcastic response, take it on the chin, learn from it, and recognise that they would probably have reacted far more positively if you'd invested more in the relationship to start with.

Send them a hand-written card in a quality envelope using a first-class stamp. I've sent many cards with motivational quotes on the front and 'hoping business is good for you' or a positive comment about something I've seen on their website or LinkedIn profile written inside. I've also sent cartoons I've cut from the paper with the words 'saw this and thought of you'. Trust me, done the right way, not too frequently but consistently, this approach is well received by customers. There's nothing more satisfying than meeting with a customer and seeing your card standing on top of their filing cabinet, book shelf or pinned to their white board.

I also use this method with prospects to thank them for their time if we've had a particularly constructive face-to-face meeting.

Send them industry information that you think will help them and their organisation. Chances are they may not be as prolific at researching the market as you are, so sending them relevant updates is a great way of keeping you on the radar. Better still, write a post and share it with them – demonstrate that you're an industry expert. They'll not only share your words internally and become your connector within their organisation, they're likely to promote you within their social network and create the process of referral. If you give them value that makes them look good, they'll share it with others.

"Think Rushworth. What did you do different that month?"

Depending on how close the working relationship is, you may **decide to arrange a tour for some of your customers' staff to visit your company** and see first-hand how you produce the goods and services that they buy from you. Traditionally, this visit would only happen between buyer and seller, but by opening up to a wider audience, let's say your customer's sales team, you could well encourage them to become advocates promoting your company.

Organise social events between your two companies. In the past, I've been involved in football, softball and cricket matches which were not only great fun on the day, but delivered useful new relationships in existing accounts that helped reverse a potential loss of business.

The bottom line is this: you cannot work with the unwilling. They will cost you time, money and even your job, and those commodities are too precious to waste. Decide who in your network you need to gain willing cooperation from and invest in them with regular and helpful deposits so that when you need to make a withdrawal, you have plenty of emotional funds set aside, earning interest and ready to pay out.

STICKING POINTS

- **Create a list of the twelve key relationships you believe will deliver the best possible chance of sales success.** These may be people within your own organisation.

- **Assign an 'attitude of gratitude' strategy to each one.** Implement the activity on a consistent timeframe to deliver an increase in cooperation.

- **Measure the return on each approach you use.** Stop any that bring no or a negative response and roll out those that work. This is a science, not an art, so use facts rather than theory.

Chapter Fourteen

Do You Take Care Of Me?

There's a book called *Your Simple Path* written by a friend of mine, Ian Tucker. Ian's book helps to bring a sense of calm to an often busy and chaotic life and allows us to find happiness in the simple things we often take for granted. Within the book is a chapter title which I've borrowed: 'Do You Take Care Of Me?' which describes an imaginary meeting between you and your younger self, or 'Little You' as Ian calls it, at the end of your first day at primary school. Little You asks whether life has been kind to you over the years, and the conversation centres around the Golden Rules that the teacher has told Little You to adopt daily as the key to a happy life.

Think about the things you are doing daily that improve your emotional resilience and sales motivation. What are you doing differently that gives you the advantage? I saw a LinkedIn poll recently where the single biggest training need for sales professionals aged twenty-five to fifty was identified as 'staying motivated and attitude' with 37% of the votes. Second was 'handling objections' with 25%, and 'closing' came third with 23%. This evidence suggests that in exactly the same way the world of professional sports has fully embraced the importance and advantage of performance psychology, so too can the world of business. But you don't have to wait for your employer; personal motivation is something you can create in a very short space of time yourself, without the need for a PhD in Psychology.

Please answer this question: in life, is there anything at all you have to do?

The logical response may be, 'Of course I do. For a start, I have to pay the rent/mortgage', but think about it a little longer. Do you *actually* have to pay your rent or could you live in a tent instead? How about obey the law, do you have to do that? Most people have on occasions driven slightly faster than the legal speed limit, and in doing so provided practical evidence that you don't have to obey the law. What about work? Do you have to work or could you give it up and take your chances on the streets?

Agreed, there are some pretty dire consequences for not doing certain things – like being homeless or ending up in prison. The big point I want to make is that you have a choice in everything, and it's you who decides what you do. You *choose* to pay your rent or mortgage because you don't want to be homeless. You *choose* to obey the law because you don't want to go to prison. No one has the power to make you do anything you don't want to do.

You possibly know someone who hates their job. They bitch, whine and complain about it every day. They probably hate their boss too, and don't get them started on their customers. People like this think they have to go to work at a place they don't enjoy for a boss they don't like. They don't yet know the difference between being responsible and taking responsibility. In fact, very few people do.

Imagine waking with a headful of have tos, got tos and must dos. Does that sound like a day you're familiar with? Does it sound like the sort of day you would enjoy? In contrast, imagine waking up to a day where everything you do is your choice and you get to decide exactly how you spend it – sound good? Well, guess what – you're already in it. *Everything* you do is your choice.

Because of that simple fact, you can take full responsibility for what you do in life and approach your sales role knowing that you don't have to do it. Instead you have decided to do it. That brings a totally different level of mindset and motivation. Imagine working for a company where everyone knows they don't have to work, they choose to. Wow. What impact would that have on staff morale and productivity?

Imagine then taking that workplace culture and adding a raft of ideas and strategies to it to boost motivation to even higher levels.

Here are tips from ten outstanding sales professionals and entrepreneurs to inspire and increase your level of sales motivation:

1. Jordan Belfort – 'Take action'. It's obvious and that's why it's first on the list. I strongly encourage you to use the variety of cognitive skills and strategies in *Sales Glue* to improve your mindset and attitude, but these reinforce and drive the action you take, not replace it. Adopt a 10x approach to your sales and do ten times the activity you would normally do in exchange for ten times the results you're used to.

2. Brian Tracy – 'Don't quit'. Another obvious one, but so important. Not every new technique you put into practice is going to work for you first time; failure is all part of the process. The secret is to keep trying the things you believe in, even if they fail the first time out, and you will ultimately succeed.

3. Warren Buffett – 'Read, read, read'. You have exactly the same amount of time in your day as a self-made guy with a 2016 $67billion net worth. The great news is that you are devoting some of those hours to reading, and that's where you will find the wisdom and inspiration to keep you ahead of the pack. I encourage you to use the time you spend in the car to listen audio books from sales experts like Tom Hopkins and Jeffrey Gitomer to expand your knowledge.

4. Gary Vaynerchuk – 'Do things that matter'. Delegate anything that must be done, but doesn't need to be done by you. Not everything on your to do list matters – most things don't. Can you become more disciplined and do only value added activity? Try it; drop stuff. If it's important, it will come back and find you. The more time you spend on things that matter, the more you'll reap the benefits associated with them.

5. Tony Robbins – 'Pay attention to the little things'. Success doesn't happen overnight; it takes time to apply and benefit from the tips in books like *Sales Glue*. Failure happens the same way: that call you didn't make; the missed follow-up; the customer you haven't spoken to for six months who has just left you. Sales success is thinking, feeling and doing all the little things that matter over and over again – value and act on every one of them.

6. Simon Sinek – 'Find your why'. All sales people know what they sell. Some even know how they sell. But very few know why they sell. Why do you work in this profession? What is it about your product and service that gets you out of bed each day? It's not for the money – that's the result of doing what you do. Find out your sales why and incorporate more of it into your communication with your prospects and customers.

7. Steve Jobs – 'Build around customers'. How easy is it for your customers to do business with you? Have you asked them? Start with the customer experience – be that your product or service or how you interact with them – and work backwards. Make it so easy for them to give you an order that they won't go anywhere else.

8. Grant Cardone – 'Always have a target'. Whether it's your pipeline, your Top 15 prospect list, your sales budget or your conversion rate, always have a target. If you aim at nothing, you'll be sure to hit it every time. Sales success is a science based on facts. Measure the outcome and results will follow.

9. Elon Musk – 'Focus on signal over noise'. Is everything you are doing in your quest for progress and improvement helping make you a better sales professional? If something isn't, stop doing it.

10. Mark Zuckerberg – 'Get feedback'. As you develop and improve through introducing new sales ideas and disciplines, you are going to change. You'll become more creative, more efficient with your time, possibly more driven and certainly more resourceful. It's important to get feedback from those you seek cooperation from to ensure that you are still seen as the one who provides them with value.

STICKING POINTS

- **If you don't already, use the dead time in your car to listen to podcasts of your favourite sales gurus.** My personal favourite is 'Sell or Die with Jeffery Gitomer'. Why not laugh while you learn?

- **Prioritise your to do list by taking the three most important 'must do by you' tasks and throwing away the rest.** Focus only on these, and when they're completed, write a new list and repeat the process. This gets you focusing only on the things that matter rather than wandering on to other less important tasks.

- **Ask your peers to give you honest feedback about how you act and behave around them.** Let them know you value their opinion and guarantee that you will not take anything they say personally – you want to improve with their help.

Conclusion

I can't know where your thoughts are as you complete this book, but I for one feel privileged to work in the sales industry. As sales professionals, our primary responsibility is to help people make a decision so that they can buy things that are right for them, solve a problem and gain genuine benefit. I'm proud to do that. My objective when writing *Sales Glue* was to inspire sales professionals to become the very best they can be at helping people buy, and I hope I have in some way inspired you to put into practice what you've read.

It's been said many times before, but let's just remind ourselves of the importance of selling: everyone in life sells, whether they're a sales person helping businesses to evolve and prosper or a school teacher trying to influence a child into learning and handing in homework on time.

If people didn't have the ability to listen, understand, build empathy, help and gain commitment, the world would grind to a halt, stuck in a state of economic paralysis. The more you invest in your own development, learning ways to improve how you sell, the more that investment will pay back with interest.

Sales Cures All.

Mark Cuban

This book wasn't written to motivate you. It cannot. Only you can motivate you. Your challenge is to take what you've learnt and tap into the way your brain naturally functions to make it a habit. Everything I've shared in these pages has brought me exactly that – sales habits. The glue that makes sales success stick. I want you to benefit in the same way, but you have to make that happen.

There are 1,440 minutes in a day. Everyone gets exactly the same amount of time as everyone else; no one gets an advantage. What each individual does have though is the ability to decide how to spend their time. When you wake each morning, almost a third of your day has already gone, and you'll spend another third of your day at work, which brings home just how little time you get each day to spend on you. This underlines the importance of doing a job that you enjoy, or having the courage to change it until you find one that does satisfy your career aspirations – your why. If you don't already, my encouragement to you is to start placing real value on your time. It truly is the most precious resource we are blessed with. Use it in worthwhile ways that bring you enjoyment, satisfaction and fulfilment, and enable you to really experience what life has to offer.

In writing *Sales Glue*, I recognised that I had a responsibility to make it an enjoyable and interesting read, but also to create something relevant and useful. I hope *Sales Glue* has achieved that for you. If it has planted some seeds in your mind that you will cultivate into long-term, productive sales habits, then please may I ask you for a small favour? If I've solved a sales problem for you, or at least contributed to the solution, would you be kind enough to tweet me with a message? I'd love to hear from you and find out what tips and ideas you have taken from the book and are working for you.

Twitter: @salesglue
#makeitstick

I wish you good luck with your next steps and hope you achieve everything you want from your career. Go and make your new skills a habit. If you do, sales success will find you, and it will stick.

And just in case you are still wondering what the vital ingredient that makes sales success stick is – it's you!

> ### *If you think you can or think you can't, either way you're probably right!*
> **Henry Ford**

Acknowledgements

There are a number of people who I want to thank for helping me write this book. Some directly, others indirectly, but each played their part.

Firstly, my wife Sue and my son Ollie, whose lives were interrupted by my decision to walk away from the comfort of corporate life. You don't yet realise the true value you brought to me with your support, but I can promise you both that you will.

Our parents, for their support in the start-up phase of my business. My father in-law Derek who lent me the 'dream car', my mother Judith and her glass-half-full approach to life, and especially my father Ray who influenced me during my informative years with the words of 'If' by Rudyard Kipling.

Gavin Drake for giving me the opportunity to work for myself, which sparked the idea for *Sales Glue*; and Phil Moran for his encouragement, humour and practical advice during the project.

I'm incredibly grateful to my publisher Rethink Press. Lucy, Joe and Alison have been instrumental in taking my story and helping me put it out there – my advice to anyone thinking of writing a book is to engage with these people, they are experts. As too is Esther Ling, my photographer, Fergus O'Donoghue who co-designed the Sales Glue image, and Ian Tucker for his kind words on the book cover and his humour.

Finally, I thank the guys whose words I read and listen to daily – Grant, Jeffrey, Peter, Tom, Phil, Zig, Ben, Jim, Brian, Darren, Pat and Sean. Thank you for the inspiration.

The Author

Matt founded his company Psyko in 2014 and joined Mindspan Global Ltd as a Director in 2015. His work centres around helping individuals and the organisations they represent to achieve more. He helps his clients improve their performance by positively impacting the cognitive skills that influence behaviour via 1-2-1 coaching and team training programmes.

Matt has clocked-up over twenty years of sales experience across a variety of industries and roles, ranging from global corporate B2B relationship management through to owner/start-up lead generation. It's this far-reaching awareness and understanding of how people buy, and the impact performance psychology has on that outcome, that allows Matt to guide sales professionals in helping more people to buy from them on a repeatable and enjoyable basis.

His final role before moving from the corporate world to running his own business, was as European Sales Director for a large multi-national packaging manufacturer. Matt had overall responsibility for a team of sales people spanning the UK and BNLX, looking after €70m of sales revenue. The decision to leave a twenty-year career behind was motivated by the desire to find a career that would both match his skills and allow him to achieve his full potential.

Matt also helps clients improve their performance skills; this work takes him through various industry and manufacturing sectors. He is currently working within the Health & Safety sector, radically improving the positive impact of Behavioural Safety training.

To get in touch with Matt, contact:
    www.salesgluebook.com
    Twitter: @salesglue
    Instagram: SalesGlue

Printed in Great Britain
by Amazon